THE HOLINESS OF
EVERYDAY LIFE

THE

HOLINESS

OF

EVERYDAY

LIFE

Joan B. MacDonald

Deseret Book Company
Salt Lake City, Utah

Library of Congress Cataloging-in-Publication Data

MacDonald, Joan B., 1946–
    The holiness of everyday life / Joan B. MacDonald
      p.   cm.
    Includes bibliographical references and index.
    ISBN 0-87579-938-8
    1. Spiritual life—Mormon Church. 2. Mormon Church—Membership.
3. Church of Jesus Christ of Latter-day Saints—Membership.
I. Title.
BX8656.M29   1995
248.4'89332—dc20   95-19817
                                                   CIP

Printed in the United States of America

10 9 8 7 6 5 4 3 2 1

He made from one
every nation of men to live on all the face of the earth
having determined allotted periods
and the boundaries of their habitation—
that they should seek God,
in the hope that they might feel after Him and find Him.
Yet He is not far from each one of us, for
"In Him we live and move and have our being,"
as even some of our poets have said,
"For we are indeed His offspring."

—ACTS 17:26–28, RSV

CONTENTS

PREFACE

Once upon a time, there was a gospel doctrine class. The course of study was the Old Testament. The teacher was discussing the Tabernacle and the Holy of Holies. She moved on to the subject of holiness in general and feeling the presence of the Holy Ghost in particular. She then posed these questions to the class: "Why don't we feel the Spirit more often? What gets in the way?" A student in the class instantly shouted out his response: "Life!" Other class members quickly added to the discussion: "Dishes in the sink! Traffic on the way to work! Kids quarreling in the kitchen! Too much to do and too little time!"

Although I understood, I had to raise my hand to disagree. After all, how can we learn the value of cleanliness, order, or nourishment without meal preparation and dishes in the sink? How can we learn to be patient without situations that require patience? How can we learn love, long-suffering, and endurance without children quarreling in the kitchen? How can we learn about priorities and what we truly value without too much to do and too little time? Life does not get in the way; life shows the way.

This book is about life. It's about the mundane and routine. It's about housework and jobs, family and friends.

This book is also about holiness. It's about those things that are sacred. It's about spiritual growth. It's about walking with the Savior and letting the Savior walk with us.

Most important, this book is about how these two things, the secular and the sacred, intertwine, support, and sustain each other.

PART 1: WORK

Chapter 1: Work

Work is sacred . . . not only because it is the fruit of self-denial, patience and toil, but because it uncovers the soul of the worker.

—HAMILTON W. MABIE

Work, work, work. It would be glorious to see mankind at leisure for once.

—HENRY DAVID THOREAU

I LOVE SUNDAYS. I love the rush of getting ready, the bustle of dressing up, my husband making pancakes in the kitchen, my daughters looking radiant, and my sons in ties passing the sacrament. I love organ music, singing loud, and visiting with friends. Most of all, I love listening to, discussing, and thinking about spiritual principles, higher values, and eternal truths. During the sacrament I reflect, evaluate, and reassess. How am I doing? Often, not as well as I'd like. But this week, I promise myself, I'll do better. I've promised to remember the Savior, and this week I will. No matter what, Lord, this week I will remember you.

Then comes Monday morning. Monday follows Sunday like the tail on a dog. I keep thinking maybe someday it won't, but it always does. And on Monday morning, life gets hard. The bustle of getting ready for church on Sunday is like a movie scene in slow motion compared to Monday. Weekday mornings are always chaotic—too many people need to use the bathroom at the same time; do all the kids have their lunch?; Danny needs a check for music lessons; who will drive Adam's project to school? Whether we're hurrying off to a job, racing to get to school on time, or facing a mountain of laundry and the leftover mess from the weekend, Monday morning hits us like a runaway train. I always find that on Mondays, by noon or before, I've forgotten. I've forgotten what seemed so urgent just the day before. I've forgotten Christ. I've not just forgotten that, somehow, I want him to be Lord of my whole life (not just my Sunday mornings); I've forgotten him altogether. Thoughts of God, Christ, scripture, or church don't even occur to me. This workaday week is such another world, a world totally other. The pace is other, the priorities are other, what matters and what doesn't, who matters and who doesn't, what I need to do and how I need to be while I'm doing it—all are other. It's as if we go to sleep Sunday night on a ranch in Wyoming and wake up Monday morning in downtown Manhattan. And we wonder: Which world is real?

Which world is most important? Are these two worlds related at all?

If so, why do they feel so separate? Why is moving from one to another so jarring?

Is it possible to integrate the spirit of Sunday into the world of Monday through Saturday?

How? Given the hectic nature of each day, how do we remember even to try?

For me, the question became, Is there some way work itself can remind me to remember? I was thrilled to discover that the answer is yes—a resounding, even thundering yes! Moreover, I believe work can be more than a reminder of lessons learned on Sunday; work has lessons of its own to teach. If we allow it, what we learn on Sunday will inform and affect what we do and learn Monday through Saturday. Likewise, what we do and learn Monday through Saturday informs and affects our experiences on Sunday. "The spirit and the body are the soul of man." (D&C 88:15.) The Sabbath and the workday, the sacred and the secular, are the soul of our lives. Though they often feel separate, different, other, *they are not*. All things are spiritual to the Lord. If I am to become more like my Heavenly Father, then all things must be spiritual to me also.

Before discussing how work can be more spiritual, I think it would be helpful to look at the nature of work—what it is and what it isn't.

The requirement to work was punishment given to Adam and Eve for their transgression in the Garden of Eden, and it *was* punishment. From ancient times to the present, millions of human beings have been forced, either through slavery or harsh economic circumstances, to work at jobs that were brutal and cruel or mindless and boring. Consider these remarks from *Working*, by Studs Terkel: "This book being about work, is, by its very nature, about violence—to the spirit as well as to the body."[1] You may think that sentiments such as those are found only "out there, in the world," but in a discussion on women in the workplace by Victor L. Brown, Jr., we read this: "Most working women, like most working men, will likely have marginal jobs with marginal pay and marginal satisfactions. Very few working people of either sex sit at large desks and enjoy high status, flexible hours, and lavish salaries; .002 percent of the general population are attorneys, .04 percent are business managers, and .0011 percent are life and physical scientists. Women's percentage of prestigious jobs is even less. Even if women could be granted fifty percent representation in high prestige professions, the majority of women (and men) would still have grinding, boring, and marginal employment."[2]

That is not just true of work for pay. It is true of housework and schoolwork as well. All types of work contain elements of personal insult and violence to body and spirit, all contain elements of drudgery and boredom, and all are, at times, only marginally satisfying. However, that is not the whole truth about work, for all types of work can also be deeply satisfying.

Elder Bruce R. McConkie wrote in *Mormon Doctrine:* "Work is the great basic principle which makes all things possible both in time and in eternity. . . . *Work is a blessing that brings salvation, idleness a curse that assures damnation.*"[3]

We've heard many a sermon along those lines. From the late eighteenth century to the end of the industrial revolution, writers like Samuel Johnson, Ralph Waldo Emerson, and Benjamin Franklin have extolled the virtues of work.

Is work a sacred activity that both develops and reveals our souls? Or is work grinding and boring, leaving body, mind, and soul heavy and numb?

I think we can safely say it is both. Work *is often* dull, repetitive, stressful, and marginally fulfilling. However, being without work is also dull and stressful and can hardly be seen as fulfilling or satisfying. Moreover, work and how we respond to the demands of work does develop and reveal our souls. Some types or work are inherently more effective at developing and revealing souls: medicine, teaching, parenting, creative work, and particularly relevant or stimulating schoolwork, for example. However, those types of work still contain elements of drudgery. Likewise, jobs that seem inherently dull or mundane, such as assembly line work or heavy manual labor, still have the capacity to develop and reveal the soul of the worker. How does work develop and reveal our souls? Knowing that work can help us in that way, how can we enlarge the development and benefit from the revealing?

To answer those questions, I can only refer to my own experience. I have a master's degree in microbiology, have worked both full-time and part-time in various hospital laboratories, have been both a full-time and part-time housewife, and am the mother of six children, so I have had some experience with every area I will be discussing. Moreover, I have looked for spiritual lessons and experienced at least some spiritual growth in every work situation in which I have engaged.

On the Job

The first lessons I learned from work on the job grew out of the discipline inherent in employment. All who successfully hold a job for an extended time have learned to report to a specified place at a specified time to perform a specified task. Moreover, the task to be performed is usually spelled out for us, we know when we have completed the task, and it is often fairly easy to evaluate the quality of our performance. That is in stark contrast to work we do in other areas of our lives, particularly the relationship work required in marriage and parenting. The simplicity of the discipline inherent in work is useful in several ways. The discipline work forces upon us is external and relatively rigid. We have to go whether we feel like it or not. Once there, we perform certain tasks. We perform them well or poorly, begrudgingly or with enthusiasm, but perform them we must. Through the years, we learn we can do more than we might have thought. Through the years, we learn we can keep going even when tired. Through the years, our work takes on a rhythm, a pace and personality of its own. Over time, we begin to use what we have learned of our own rhythm, pace, consistency, and achievement to structure for ourselves a more disciplined personal life. Personal scripture study, prayer, Church callings, friendships, and family relationships all benefit from habits developed at work.

Another way work can advance our spiritual strength and growth is through the lessons we learn there about the quest for excellence. Two things occur in the workplace that help us learn to improve performance: one is annual job evaluations connected to pay raises, and the other is the struggle for advancement. Evaluations, if we allow them, can teach us techniques for self-evaluation, can teach us about our strengths and weaknesses, and can teach us a great deal about how others view us. Ambition and desire for advancement can teach us about effort, hard work, attention to detail, and the value of continuing education. We can apply all these values and skills in other areas of our lives, from relationships to Church service to personal spiritual study and growth.

Finally, work provides numerous opportunities for developing honesty and personal integrity. Although a job often provides a fair amount of structure and external discipline, most jobs provide flexibility within that structure. We are all familiar with the admonition to provide an honest day's work for an honest day's pay. We are also aware of the many ways work can be avoided, circumvented, or prolonged in the workplace. At work we can learn to give our best and do our best regardless of the circumstances or consequences. At work we have daily opportunities to cut corners or not, to cover mistakes or admit them and correct them promptly, to pay close attention to detail and quality, or to give the least amount required by the job. Making these daily, hourly choices in favor of honesty, integrity, and the best we can do is nothing less than calisthenics for the soul, making work a wonderful opportunity to build and develop character.

Revealing Ourselves—Revealing God

Discipline, evaluation, striving for excellence, and developing personal integrity—these are common experiences of the workplace that help develop character. But developing character isn't enough. I said at the beginning that work can develop and reveal our souls. A soul is more than character. To develop one's soul implies a deep spiritual effort, and to be spiritual implies a connection to God.

Many people, both in and out of the Church, hunger for a deeper connection to God in their daily lives. How do we get that connection? What are we really after? Why do we sometimes hurry through busy days, wondering, "Is this all there is?" I don't know about you, but I need more. I need meaning and I need God shining through and revealing himself around me. I think most of us do. We need to see, understand, and experience God. We also need to know and understand ourselves. We want to know our strengths and our weaknesses, why we do what we do, and how we can do better. Finally, we want to know that these two things connect. We want to know that God loves and accepts us as we are, and we want to experience him helping us become even better, every day and in every situation. We are in luck, because the revealing of God, of ourselves, and of the connection between ourselves and God occurs all around us, and it occurs a lot at work. The key to seeing it is awareness.

We start by becoming aware of what work teaches us about ourselves. Do we approach our work eagerly or reluctantly? Are we fast or slow, careful or sloppy? What do we do well? Are we kind or harsh, encouraging or critical? If we but pay attention to what we do and how we are while we are doing it, we can learn a great deal about ourselves. As we work at this learning and then at improving, we can invite our Heavenly Father into the process to help us bring our behavior and attitudes closer to his. Once we start inviting our Heavenly Father into our efforts at work, we have done a great thing—we have started to think about God while we are at work. We have opened our minds and thus our consciousness to the possibility of God's presence in the workplace. Then we are ready for the next step, looking for ways God might reveal himself to us at work.

We are accustomed to thinking of God as revealing himself through prayer, scripture study, dreams and visions, and even history—but through work? Well, of course. We need only remember how God reveals himself most often. Think of Moses, Joseph Smith, Abraham, Lehi, Nephi, Ruth, Mary, your bishop, or your visiting teacher; God most often reveals himself through the lives, actions, and words of people. Workplaces are therefore a veritable treasure-house. They are not only filled with people, but they are also filled with many different *kinds* of people. Work is often the only place where we are exposed to any cultural diversity. Because of that diversity, God can reveal himself to us in new and sometimes surprising or challenging ways.

I live in a ward in the suburbs of Boston. Over the years I've seen six or seven bishops come and go. Most of them have been successful businessmen. Many of them have been required to travel extensively in relation to their work. I remember two of them relating stories of personal encounters in foreign lands that profoundly affected their spiritual lives. One bishop told of spending a week in Mexico with a Mexican executive and his family. The man was highly successful, wealthy, powerful, intelligent, and articulate. He was also a devout Catholic and was deeply committed to his family. He led his family in daily devotions, actively taught his children, and often made sacrifices at work to make time for his family. He and our bishop had several long discussions about the importance of the family and the need to keep work and family commitments in balance. The second bishop spent a week in India with a similarly successful Hindu man. They also spent time discussing the importance of devotion to God and family. In addition, they discussed the responsibility of wealth and position. Our bishop discovered that his Hindu counterpart was deeply involved in helping solve some of India's social problems. Both bishops came home from their travels humbled and challenged to increase their commitments to the Lord and to their families.

Cultural diversity can also result in exposure to ideas, perspectives, and ways of being that we might not otherwise encounter or consider. Diversity can challenge us to alter or expand our world view, to reassess our understanding of how God works with *all* of his children. It can shed a fresh new light on basic assumptions with which we've become overly comfortable. Finally, diversity can bring us face-to-face with people who, without the benefit of the Church, have reached a level of spiritual maturity that dwarfs our own and through whom we might suddenly see the essence of true religion. We may be meeting in a conference room, conversing with a friend during our morning break, lecturing in front of a class, or laying pipe at a construction site when something is said or done, and—surprise!—like Paul on the road to Damascus or Jacob in the desert wrestling with an angel, we see something we never saw before, understand something we never understood before, or have a problem we never had before. Because nonmembers and non-Christians express themselves with different words or interpret their experiences in different ways, or, sometimes, because their experiences or understanding are so similar to ours even though they are not members of the Church, they can open our minds and hearts to new ideas, new feelings, or new insights and understanding. They can even open our minds and hearts to see God.

As I said before, I work in a hospital laboratory. The hospital is large, but the laboratory is isolated, with only fifteen employees. Among them are several agnostics, an atheist, two born-again Christians, three Jews, a Muslim, and a Hindu.

One of them is a woman who works full-time, has three children, is a liberal Unitarian, and, in spite of her busy schedule, bakes bread once a month and takes it to a shelter for homeless women in downtown Boston.

One of them is a woman who works part-time, has two children, and attends school part-time earning a degree in landscape architecture. Several years ago she volunteered her time to design and help plant a garden outside the hospital's Cancer Care Center. Each year she supervises volunteers in planting hundreds of bulbs in the garden.

One of them is a born-again Christian who is a former drug addict and homosexual. She now teaches a Bible study group at a local prison each week. She taught me more about the relationship between grace and works than dozens of Sunday School lessons.

All three Jewish people who work on my shift make it a point to volunteer to work on Christmas and Easter so their Christian co-workers can have those days off.

My view of history was deepened in a discussion with a Jewish co-worker who had lived in Israel for several years.

I was introduced to a wealth of wonderful spirit-centered books through people at work. Because of co-workers, I have read such authors as Madeline L'Engle, Polly Berends, C. S. Lewis, and Frederich Beuchner.

It was a Catholic co-worker who helped a technician on the verge of a nervous breakdown one night. When I complimented her later, she said, "My heart just went out to her. What else could I do?" She taught me how to be responsive to need.

One winter we had an inordinate amount of backbiting and gossip in the lab between two cliques. I watched a co-worker "clique-hop" back and forth between the two groups, smoothing things out. She taught me what it means to be a peacemaker. Time and time again at work, my understanding of what it means to live the gospel, to follow Christ, and to be a child of God has been redefined, expanded, and enlarged. It is through these experiences of diverse people from diverse backgrounds that I have come to understand the truth of the scripture in Acts that opens this book: "He made from one *all nations* of men; that they might seek God!"

As an aside I want you to know that the people who have

taught me these wonderful lessons are the same ones who occasionally swear or tell dirty stories. Do I mind? Well, maybe I do now and then, but I love these people. I cherish what they have taught me. I value who I have become because of their example. And in their lives and their stories, I see the hand of God.

Defining Values

Jobs, which demand so much of our time and often draw forth our deep emotional commitment, challenge us to define our values and establish our priorities. Those who work forty hours a week or more will never equally balance work, family, and church in terms of time. However, a balance must be struck in terms of value and priority. We must not compromise our values in order to succeed at work. We must not sacrifice our family relationships in order to succeed at work. And, finally, we must remain conscious of our values and priorities while we are at work. Work takes up the bulk of our time, attention, study, planning, and goal setting. Family, church, and spiritual matters can become inconvenient distractions, whining around our ears like mosquitoes in the night. When they become sufficiently annoying, we impatiently slap at them before returning our attention to our work. Work and career can become so important to us that even personal values can be pushed aside as we rush after the goal of success. Hugh Nibley describes the dangers of compromising values for the sake of the job in this discussion of careers:

> Careerism is the determination to reign in hell rather than serve in heaven. "From the moment a person starts treating his life as a career, worry is his constant companion. . . . Careerism results not only in constant anxiety, but also in an underdeveloped heart. . . . The careerist constantly betrays himself, since he must ignore idealistic, compassionate and courageous impulses that might jeopardize his career."
>
> "Perfect love casts out all fear," said the Lord, but who wants that if it jeopardizes one's career? Satan's

promise to split Adam and Eve was accomplished
when God declared, "My people have sold themselves
for gold and silver."[4]

When work and career become our top priority; when our
jobs, which already consume so much of our time, also become
the focus of all our attention, we are in trouble. Moreover, this is
an easy trap to fall into. How do we avoid it? How do we strike a
balance? The solution is simple to state though difficult to
achieve. The solution is to bring a spiritual focus into our everyday lives. I believe we must bring the Savior to work with us.

The Prophet Micah tells us how to go about serving God. He
declares that we do not serve God in our temples with our offer-
ings, rituals, or prayers:

> Wherewith shall I come before the Lord, and bow
> myself before the high God? Shall I come before him
> with burnt offerings, with calves of a year old? Will
> the Lord be pleased with thousands of rams, or with
> ten thousands of rivers of oil? [Or with perfect sacra-
> ment meeting attendance or hundreds of endowments
> performed?] Shall I give my firstborn for my transgres-
> sion, the fruit of my body for the sin of my soul? He
> hath showed thee, O man, what is good; and what
> doth the Lord require of thee, but to do justly, and to
> love mercy, and to walk humbly with thy God.
>
> (MICAH 6:6–8.)

Where are we to do justly—only at church on Sunday? When
are we to love mercy—only when we are home teaching? How
can we ever learn to walk humbly with God if we don't do it
every day? Forty hours a week, at work, we must do justly. Forty
hours a week, at work, we must seek mercy. Forty hours a week,
we must humbly invite God to walk with us.

Work, whether at home or in a job, provides us with a great
opportunity to choose God. If we lived in a monastery and spent
our days in scripture study and prayer, it would all be so easy. That

is not what God has asked us to do. He has placed us in the world. Work provides the perfect setting to meet that challenge. The very tension work creates, the very attraction to be career-focused, is the very opportunity to choose God and to actively demonstrate the depth of our commitment to serve him above all else.

Our former stake president is W. Mitt Romney, son of George Romney. In the fall of 1994 he ran a political campaign in an effort to unseat Ted Kennedy. Because of Kennedy's prominence, the campaign was thoroughly covered in the media, with many news-paper articles on Mitt Romney. It was interesting to see how many of those articles focused on Romney's personal life. It was even more interesting to see what they revealed. Although highly suc-cessful and very busy, President Romney would start many of his days with hospital visits to sick members of the Church. His calen-dar book not only noted business and church appointments but also events in the lives of his wife and children. He even kept track of how many nights he was away from home for his children's bed-time, making sure they were not too many and that he was regu-larly at home in the evening to be with his children. Here is a man who has used the tension between work and other values to declare and deepen his commitment to the Lord and to his family.

Finally, even without character development, exposure to diversity, and helping to define values, work is spirit-filled; in fact, the process of work glows from within like rocks touched by the finger of God. I firmly believe that everything we do contains an underlying spiritual principle. I wonder about work. What could it be? What spiritual principle underlies and shines through work? Is work about faith? No. Charity? Not usually. Purity? No. Order? Sometimes, not always. Beauty? No. Power? Yes. That's it, isn't it. Work requires and calls forth our power to do, to create (both objects and ideas), to identify and solve prob-lems, to foresee and evaluate consequences for good or evil, and to make decisions and choices. Are these powers attributes of God? Yes! Do we become more like God when we develop these powers in ourselves and use them for good? Yes! Will we need these powers in the celestial kingdom, where we will create worlds without end? Yes! Work *is* sacred! With the help of the Lord, our work can help sanctify and exalt us. Welcome, welcome, Monday morning. Go work.

Housework

It has been my experience that housework presents a whole different set of learning experiences than working outside the home. There is no external structure or discipline to work done at home; the structure and discipline must come from within. There is almost never a sense that the job is done, no external performance evaluations, and no opportunity for promotion or advancement. There is also no inherent exposure to cultural diversity; indeed, working at home is often a lonely job and needs to be accompanied by time away to be with friends and neighbors. On the other hand, full-time homemaking offers flexibility and a level of freedom not found in any other job. Moreover, I have found that the nature of housework itself offers some solutions to its own unique problems.

The Myth of Balancing

During a spiritual living lesson, a mother of young children raised her hand and complained of her life. "How do I do it?" she asked. "How do I find the time for scripture study and prayer when home and family demands press upon me so? From early morning until late at night, the demands of housework and children seem ever present. How can I strike a balance? Where can I fit in what I need to do to promote my own spiritual growth?"

Many Latter-day Saints struggle with those questions. In *Gift from the Sea*, Anne Morrow Lindbergh beautifully expresses her own struggles: "The problem is not merely Woman and Career, Woman and the Home, Woman and Independence. It is basically, how to remain whole in the midst of the distractions of life."[5]

How do we remain whole in the midst of the distractions of

life? In her book, Lindbergh suggests the importance of finding space and time for solitude. As important as solitude is, it is not always possible. The truth is, women with several young children *are* often busy from early morning until late at night. Even if a woman is sufficiently well organized to find a few moments to herself, those moments must often be used to get needed rest. Although Relief Society teachers may quote "To every thing there is a season," that thought offers little reassurance to women whose lives are out of balance for years on end.

For those who are well organized and disciplined enough to find space in their busy lives for solitude, there arises a second problem. Be it daily scripture study, trips to the temple, or a weekend retreat, once the period of solitude and contemplation is over, they have to come back! When I was a young mother with four children under the age of three, I was repeatedly advised by physician and friends to take time for myself—to get away from it all. Of course, it was wonderful when I could, but after the break was over I had to come back! Soon the resolutions made and peaceful feelings acquired faded away, and I was bogged down again with seemingly endless diapers, cleaning, and meals. Getting away didn't solve my problems, nor did it help me cope with life's daily demands. However, through the years, I did learn to cope—and then to grow. I did this not by getting away but by learning to see the work of the Lord in my own work. To my surprise, the *work* itself has become my most effective teacher.

What is a homemaker's work, and how can it be spiritually sustaining? The primary task of homemakers is parenting. Though often difficult and frustrating, parenting is of itself deeply meaningful and profoundly spiritual. The second task of the homemaker is maintaining the home—housework. Housework is not usually thought of as inherently meaningful, and, at least at first glance, it is hardly spiritually sustaining. In fact, when it comes to living a spiritual life, housework just seems to get in the way.

The Truth Is under Here Somewhere

So many times, I've set magnificent goals and dreamed magnificent dreams only to be stopped dead in my tracks by housework. It always seems to be there. The house *always* needs *something*, the laundry never ends, and just when I think I have time to start a project, the grocery shopping needs to be done. For years I had a problem with housework. I did it reluctantly and often found myself filled with resentment and anger. "Why do I have to clean this up?" I moaned. "I didn't make this mess!" So often, it seemed everywhere I looked, I saw only clutter.

I was defeated before I even began. Even when I started my day with scripture study and prayer, I would send the Spirit flying as soon as I started cleaning up. Where was the answer to my problem?

First, let's define the problem more clearly. My problem was really a point of view. I was looking at the work before me and *seeing* several things:

1. The clutter.

2. The work and time required to clean it up.

3. The unfairness that I would be cleaning it rather than someone else (anyone—please).

4. Inadequacy: mine.

5. Carelessness: theirs.

No wonder I felt bad! To solve the problem I had several options:

1. Leave home and become a hermit. Attractive choice, don't you think? No—not practical.

2. Hire help. No—no money.

3. Buy a whip and crack it over husband and children at frequent intervals. Now there's a thought!

4. Change my viewpoint. Yechh! What would that solve? Everything.

For some women, responsible modifications of 1, 2, and 3 are viable choices. For myself, and for most other women, they are not. Putting aside feminist arguments and all the shoulds and oughts they imply, housework remains primarily the responsibility of women. That is particularly true for women who choose to be at home raising their children.

So I set about to change my viewpoint—easier said than done, no matter what the positive thinking books might lead us to believe. I had to go deeper than positive thinking. I had to change perceptions. To do that required more than positive thinking; to do that I needed understanding.

Years ago, in a college biochemistry course, I learned something important about myself. I learned how I learn. Before an exam, several students would gather to study together. While others struggled to memorize cycles and pathways, I seemed to have no problem. One night a fellow student asked for my trick. After giving it some thought, I realized I couldn't "memorize" any better than anyone else. However, I loved figuring out the way things work. I would study the cycles and pathways, trying to understand what was going on and why. Once I understood, I remembered the details. I still learn that way. The answer to my housework problem was both simple and complex. As with the biochemistry, it was easy to do once I understood. Also as with the biochemistry, the struggle was in coming to an understanding.

I started with the usual "to dos." I read the "how-to" books—many excellent ones. I got the necessary equipment. I scheduled. I organized, plotted, and planned. I read inspirational articles reminding me of the importance of my task. I still hated housework! I still felt resentful! I continued to read and talk to other women. Gradually a new understanding began to dawn. I shifted my focus away from "to do" and toward "to be." My shift started with this scripture: "Whatsoever things are true, whatsoever things are honest, whatsoever things are just, whatsoever things are pure, whatsoever things are lovely, whatsoever things are of good report; if there be any praise, if there be any virtue, *think on these things*." (Philippians 4:8; emphasis added.)

"Think on these things." OK! While I do housework I'll think about virtue and praise and loveliness. You know those positive-thinking books I mentioned earlier—the ones that give you so many easy ways to change your viewpoint? That's what came next. I read them all. Surely that would do the trick. I wrote affirmations and taped them to the bathroom mirror. *Now we're getting somewhere!* I thought. I did visualizations, picturing myself cheerfully whistling as I vacuumed an immaculate floor. I felt great while I was affirming. I felt great while I was visualizing. I felt frustrated, resentful, inadequate, and inefficient while I was cleaning! What now? Back to the scriptures!

> Hearing ye shall hear and shall not understand
> and seeing ye shall see and not perceive.
>
> (ACTS 28:26.)

Was there something here I was not perceiving? I didn't think so. All that was here was clutter, dirt, and hard work, right? Hmmm.

> The Lord seeth not as man seeth; for man looketh
> on the outward appearance.
>
> (1 SAMUEL 16:7.)

Well, there was no question I was looking on the outward appearance. Could these scriptures be applied to the homely job of housework? It seemed unlikely. These scriptures were talking about spiritual things. Housework, it seemed to me, was definitely not spiritual; mundane, temporal, worldly, sometimes even dreary, but spiritual? No, definitely not spiritual.

While I was pondering these things, I heard an interesting discussion at church. The discussion was about Joseph Smith's assertion that *all* things are spiritual. We then discussed spiritual attributes of the physical world. Some of the words used were *purity, order, simplicity, truth,* and *beauty.* Purity—order—beauty. Oh my goodness, that was it! Why hadn't I *seen* it before ("seeing ye shall see and not perceive")? The next time I cleaned, I looked. Sure enough, there they were (admittedly, not until I was done, but there nonetheless): purity (cleanliness), order, and beauty. Housework is not about dirt. Housework is not about clutter. Housework is not about time or work or energy or fatigue. Housework is not about who messed up or who cleaned up. And housework is definitely not about me! Housework is about purity, order, and beauty.

The Apostle Paul, quoting Isaiah, wrote, "The heart of this people is waxed gross, and their ears are dull of hearing, and their eyes have they closed; lest they should see with their eyes, and understand with their heart, and should be converted." (Acts 28:26.) In the sense that *converted* means changed, I was converted. I have never looked at housework in the same way again. Before, I looked at the work before me and saw five things: clutter, work, injustice, inadequacy, and carelessness. Let's go back over some of those things and look at them with new eyes.

Spiritual Principles—Practical Solutions

The first problem was the chronic clutter. The mess was there all right, and there all too often to suit me. But that is looking at the outward appearance, and we don't want to do that anymore. Trying to look at clutter with more spiritual eyes taught me two things. First, I tried to understand the nature of clutter itself— what does clutter represent? What *things* do we regard as clutter? Toys played with and not put away, dirty dishes to be washed, coats not hung up, books read and not put away. Toys, dishes, clothes, books; children, food, warmth, intelligence. Clutter is a by-product of life being lived. Clutter is a mirror reflecting some of our sweetest blessings. Go ahead—look at this mess. Look at this beautiful, wonderful mess. Thank you, Lord. Now let's tidy up.

The second thing I learned about clutter is what it is not. Unlike the spiritual qualities of purity, order, and beauty, clutter is temporal. The word *temporal* is closely related to another word: *temporary.* Clutter and dirt are temporary. Order, purity, and beauty are permanent. Always there. Always to be found. Sometimes quite buried but there nonetheless. Pick up and wash, and there they are. They were there all along. As spiritual principles, order, purity, and beauty are not only true, but they are also attributes of God himself and of the god-nature within us. As we pick up the clutter, wipe away the dirt, and beautify our homes, we are allowing those attributes freer expression. When we clean, order, and beautify our homes, we bless our homes, and our work becomes a holy work, a work that can feed our spirits and sustain our souls.

Another problem is created when we focus our attention on the work (which we may not want to do) and on how time consuming it is, mentally anticipating the completion of tasks that are never really complete! It's helpful to think of this problem as it is expressed in the workplace. Doing housework while measuring the time and effort required to do it, eagerly anticipating its completion, is like being an employee who constantly watches the clock, anticipating coffee break, lunch, and quitting time. Not only does the quality of the work suffer but so does the individual, for nothing is quite so miserable as being stuck someplace you don't want to be, doing something you don't want to do, while your mind is off someplace else. How do you feel when you let your mind do that sort of thing? Trapped, restless, miserable! Unfortunately, when the job is over and you've moved on to the much-anticipated quitting time, it's a disappointment. You've shot your whole day. This common human phenomenon of anxious anticipation for "what comes next" is insightfully and humorously described by Benjamin Hoff in *The Tao of Pooh*:

> "Ouch!" said Pooh, landing on the floor.
>
> "That's what happens when you go to sleep on the edge of the writing table," I said. "You fall off."
>
> "Just as well," said Pooh.
>
> "Why's that?" I asked.
>
> "I was having an awful dream," he said.
>
> "Oh?"
>
> "Yes. I'd found a jar of honey . . . , " he said, rubbing his eyes.
>
> "What's so awful about that?" I said.

"It kept moving," said Pooh. "They're not supposed to do that. They're supposed to sit still."

"Yes, I know."

"But whenever I reached for it, this jar of honey
would sort of go someplace else."

"A nightmare," I said.

"Lots of people have dreams like that," I added
reassuringly.

"Oh," said Pooh. "About unreachable jars of
honey?"

"About the same sort of thing," I said. "That's not
unusual. The odd thing, though, is some people live
like that."

"Why?" asked Pooh.

"I don't know," I said. "I suppose it gives them
Something to Do."

"It doesn't sound like much fun to me," said Pooh.

No, it doesn't. A way of life that keeps saying,
"Around the next corner, above the next step," works
against the natural order of things and makes it so difficult to be happy and good that only a few get to where
they would naturally have been in the first place—
Happy and Good—and the rest give up and fall by the
side of the road, cursing the World which is not to
blame but which is there to help show the way."[6]

"Around the next corner, above the next step." "When I get
this done and out of my way—once the kids are in school the
house will look better—I'll do a quick pick up, and then I can—
tomorrow, later, in the morning, next week . . . " No wonder we
become frustrated! The work never ends, and "later" never
comes. We spend a large portion of our time anticipating a quitting time that never materializes. The first step in dealing with
this problem is to stop anticipating. Instead of focusing your mind
on the time and work required to finish, focus your mind on the
task at hand. Look around. See what needs to be done. Start. As

you work, become absorbed in what you are doing, giving it your full attention. Notice the warmth and fresh smell of the fluffy clothes as you pull them from the dryer. Purity is being expressed there. As you fold the clothes, notice order emerging. As you share the task with your four-year-old (something you wouldn't be willing to do if you were in a hurry to finish), you feel harmony and peace. When the job is done, you move right on. What needs to be done next? Your mind, body, and heart become absorbed in what you're doing and in the spiritual qualities being expressed. At some point during your work, you've forgotten yourself; you've forgotten your busy schedule, your complaints, and your preoccupations.

Benjamin Hoff continues: "The honey doesn't taste so good once it is being eaten; the goal doesn't mean so much once it is reached; the reward is not so rewarding once it has been given. If we add up all the rewards in our lives, we won't have very much. But, if we add up the spaces between the rewards, we'll come up with quite a bit. And if we add up the rewards and the spaces, then we'll have everything—every minute of the time we spent. What if we could enjoy it?"[7]

What, indeed, if we could enjoy it?

Finally, I have to say that if housework is about order, purity, and beauty—and it is—and if there are spiritual satisfactions to be garnered there—and there are—then why not do much of it as a family? You might recall that the last three feelings I struggled with as I did housework were unfairness (why me?), guilt that the house got dirty in the first place, and anger at the carelessness of other family members. Those feelings are a response to real problems, and learning how to solve problems is one reason we have come to earth. Aha! Another opportunity for growth—whole family growth. A woman who stays at home to raise the children will be the one to do most of the housework simply because she is there. That does not mean, however, that she should do it all. Much can be gained when the whole family shares the responsibility. Husbands and wives learn to work together. Children learn not only the value of work but also the value of cleanliness and order. We learn best from personal experience, and children experience the same sense of satisfaction and peace that adults experience when their surroundings are orderly and they have helped create that order. Finally, families that do house and yard work together find that some of their sweetest family moments come when they are working together.

As Polly Berien Berends wrote, "Though my children are still young, I can already say that we have told more stories, sung more songs, shared more profound thoughts, exchanged more deep secrets, confessed more doubts, and received more assurance, hugged and laughed harder, and been kinder and freer and jollier together drying dishes in the kitchen than we ever have sitting at dinner or before the fire."[8]

When I walk into a room to clean, I no longer feel it is unfair that I am doing this instead of someone else. I no longer feel inadequate because the room is dirty and somehow I think it never should be. I no longer resent the rest of my family for their contributions to the disarray. I look at my home and feel glad. Even before I start, I know that purity, order, and beauty are under there somewhere. I look at any clutter on top of that purity and order, and I see blessings. How do I remain whole amid the distractions of life? One way is to reduce the distractions. Housework used to be a big distraction for me. Now housework helps me stay focused. It's like a long, drawn-out prayer of gratitude for blessings of home and family. It's an opportunity to meditate upon the spiritual qualities of our physical world. It brings peace of mind and immense satisfaction, for as I bless our home, the Lord blesses me.

School

For some the rush of Monday morning is not a rush to work or a flurry of activity within the home, each with their attendant responsibilities for the welfare of others. Students are working too, but their work is primarily on their own behalf. Students experience the same jarring differences between Sunday's spiritual focus and the demanding world of Monday through Saturday. Often those differences are even more jarring as teachers and professors seem to challenge many of the spiritual principles so highly spoken of just the day before. At least in the privacy of our own home and in the work done to earn a living, we are not faced with the daily, sometimes hourly, challenges to our most cherished beliefs. Can God be found in the classroom or on the campus? Why have the prophets stressed the importance of a good education? Is it possible for campus experiences and education to strengthen faith? Is the purpose of school just to prepare us to be self-sufficient in a complex world, or is more going on?

Throughout a student's educational experience, from kindergarten to graduate school, the primary focus is gaining information and acquiring the skills necessary to function in our complex world. Yet much more is happening during those years. Students are a little like caterpillars, spinning and weaving cocoons from which their personal butterflies will someday emerge. School, classroom discussions, teachers, and books all influence the designs and patterns expressed on the butterflies' wings. The students themselves choose and form the final designs and must be conscious and alert to the patterns forming in their minds. Their task is important. They must incorporate and integrate the knowledge the world supplies with their knowledge of the gospel; their personal experiences in the world with their personal experiences with the Spirit. In addition to the challenges and tasks schooling imposes, students are also involved in the process of growing up, physically, emotionally, and spiritually. Young people experience three aspects of growing up: separation, discovery, and definition of self.

Separation from parents and family occurs throughout childhood and adolescence and culminates when children leave home to attend college or marry. Parents and youngsters alike become increasingly aware of the children's growing independence. Once they are in college, young adults are free to choose their experiences independent of parental influences. For the first time they are truly free to choose the gospel for its own sake. No parent is present to encourage them to attend church, read scriptures, choose friends wisely, and come home on time. There is no immediate or overt disapproval if they make choices contrary to the parents' values. During this time, young people are also separating from their former immature selves. The young, naïve, unconscious self is giving birth to a more conscious, sophisticated, knowing self. School doesn't just facilitate this process; it forces it. Books, information, other students, and teachers challenge the young adults' givens in life, including spiritual givens: Jesus loves me this I know, in the beginning God created, families can be together forever, there is beauty all around—all of these and more are challenged again and again in biology, psychology, sociology, math, art, and literature classes. All the simple answers learned in Primary are challenged and exposed for what they are—simple answers. Suddenly the young people need more complete and complex answers. So they separate from what they thought they knew and from who they thought they were, not from choice but because learning forces them. This process can be painful and frightening. Parents and the Church need to be sensitive to the difficulties young people face as they go through their high school and college years. Parents, Church leaders, and young people alike need to remember one very important thing: the Church is true! Heavenly Father lives, and Jesus Christ is his son and our Savior! We need not fear. Heavenly Father will help both young people and the adults who care about them, if we but have faith. We can't allow ourselves to be too afraid of the questions education raises or the changes brought about by increasing maturity. Questions have answers, and if young people are humble and seek their Heavenly Father's help, they can allow ideas that are too simple or too naïve to die, knowing that God is with them and will help them reach new levels of understanding.

Two years ago I taught early morning seminary to a group of ten wonderful young people. We were studying the Old Testament. Of course we began with the creation. Of course there were immediate questions about evolution. I asked the students to explain to me their understanding of the theory of evolution. I was amazed to find that their understanding of Darwin was as naïve and oversimplified as a five-year-old's understanding of the gospel. "Man descended from monkeys" seemed to wrap it all up for them. A little knowledge can be a dangerous thing, a dangerous thing that more knowledge can often help. So we talked about evolution. We talked about fishes, amphibians, reptiles, birds, and mammals. We talked about missing links, not just between man and other primates but also between fishes, amphibians, reptiles, birds, and mammals. Then we talked about physics, particularly the first and second laws of thermodynamics, laws that the theory of evolution defies. Then we talked about the gospel, about what the scriptures tell us and what they leave out. We explored a wide range of ideas and teachings on the subject. We concluded there is much that science cannot tell us and much the Lord has chosen not to tell us. We simply don't know all the details. That may sound ambiguous, but it's the truth, and young people need to know the truth. More important than any conclusion we reached, we went through an important process together. We were open to the questions, explored the possible answers, and returned to our faith, realizing that the gospel is true and that some questions have answers we can find now and some don't—but the process of asking is important, for only those who seek find.

During this whole process of questioning and seeking, immature ideas and understandings must be examined, discarded, added upon, or deepened. That is true of what we learned at home, at school, and at church. It is true not because what we were taught was false but because what we were taught was appropriate for our age. Anselm of Canterbury put it this way: "It seems to me a case of negligence if, after becoming firm in our faith, we do not strive to understand what we believe." That is the task young people, after separating from parents and their own naïveté, must undertake.

The second stage is discovery, which in a spiritual context is nothing less than revelation. The ideas and information young people are exposed to in school, coupled with the insistence of teachers that they learn to think for themselves, force them to do just that—think for themselves. It is usually during this time that young people realize they cannot live on borrowed light; they must find their own. Questions raised in classrooms or dorm discussions are answered with increased time in scripture study and prayer. As long as seekers have the courage and faith to continue seeking, some answers will be found, eventually leading the seekers to God himself. Here is the opportunity for true knowing, for direct encounter with our Heavenly Father, and for personal testimony received not from others but from the Holy Ghost.

The final process school helps move along is learning to defend our beliefs in the face of dissent. Many students have already completed the stages of separation and discovery before leaving home for college. Still the challenges are great, for it requires both courage and skill to express beliefs and values clearly and firmly. The benefits are that each time we explain what we believe, our ability to do so improves and our convictions deepen.

One of my friends has a teenage daughter, Jenny, who has great faith and a strong testimony. During her junior year in high school, her English class was asked to read a book that was filled with foul language. This young girl was soon deeply offended by what she was reading. She agonized over what she should do. She discussed the problem with her parents. Finally, she approached her teacher. She carefully explained her beliefs, explaining that she couldn't read the book in good conscience. Arrangements were made for her to read *The Taming of the Shrew* instead. The reading was more difficult. Furthermore, she lost the benefit of class discussions relating to the book she was reading, resulting in a grade that was lower than usual. Nevertheless, Jen was glad she had made the choice she had. The process taught her several important lessons: She learned she had a choice. She learned what she wanted her choice to be. She learned she was capable of defending her faith to an adult authority figure. Perhaps most important, she learned she was a young woman of conviction and courage. A year later, when Jen was applying for admission to Brigham Young University, her English teacher wrote a letter of recommendation for Jen in which she recounted this story, praising Jen for her integrity. Jenny will never forget this experience. It strengthened her testimony, deepened her faith, and increased her courage, and it didn't happen Sunday morning in sacrament meeting; it happened at school.

Jobs, housework, school—secular activities all, associated with the world and worldliness; yet this is the context within which the gospel must be lived. These are the activities that consume the bulk of our time. These are our lives. Heavenly Father did not send us to earth just to mark time until we could return to him. He sent us here to learn to make choices; take responsibility; create order, purity, and beauty; and gain knowledge and understanding. He sent us here to work.

PART 2:
RELATIONSHIPS

Chapter 2: Ourselves

And the soul,
if she is to know herself,
must look
into the soul:
The stranger and the enemy, we saw him in the mirror.

—GEORGE SEFERIS

WHO ARE YOU?

Who am I?

Oh, I know, I know—I am a child of God, and so my needs are great.

But what does that mean? And if I am a child of God, why am I not more godly? And does knowing I am a child of God really answer the question "Who am I?" What is personhood and personality, and how do those concepts relate to the question of who I am? What is my personal mission here on earth, or do I even have one? These are some of the questions that flit in and out of our minds or rumble somewhere in our subconsciouses, growling like a hungry stomach.

Who are we—really?

Enemy to God or Child of God— Which or When?

The natural man is an enemy to God, and has been from the fall of Adam.

(MOSIAH 3:19.)

Beloved, now are we the sons of God, and it doth
not yet appear what we shall be: but we know that,
when he shall appear, we shall be like him; for we
shall see him as he is.

(1 JOHN 3:2.)

Natural man? Enemy to God? Or God's own beloved sons and
daughters? Or is it both; sometimes one, sometimes the other?
Which are we most of the time? Which says the most about our
essential nature? Which were we first?

First we were sons and daughters of God. We became "natural"
when we came to earth, participated in the fall, and became
proud, rebellious, and self-centered. Those "natural" tendencies
of our fallen selves are attributes we fight and struggle with all of
our lives. Moving beyond the natural man to become more and
more that which we already are, children of God, is what our life
on earth is for.

Becoming

I went to a women's discussion circle several years ago. The
leader started the discussion by having everyone in the room
introduce themselves and tell the group one thing about themselves that defined who they were. When the discussion came
back to her, she said there was only one word that accurately
described herself; that word was *becoming*.

The scriptures state that we are all children of God and that
"*it doth not yet appear what we shall be.*"

This is unsettling. "Who am I?" we ask. The scriptures answer,
You are a child of God and so you can't yet fully understand who
you are or who you are becoming. All you can know for sure is
that you are in process.

This is also liberating. We are becoming. We are not done yet.
We will never be done in this life. Awareness of this can free us
from self-imposed restrictions. We are freed from role-playing,

script-following, and self-limitations. We are led into openness: open now to all possibilities and directions, open to ideas, open to different ways of being, open to the promptings of the Spirit. All of life becomes a walk in faith. Since we do not know for sure exactly where we are going or who we are becoming, life can be lived as described in the beautiful hymn "Lead, Kindly Light":

> Lead, kindly Light, amid th'encircling gloom;
> Lead thou me on!
> The night is dark, and I am far from home;
> Lead thou me on!
> Keep thou my feet;
> I do not ask to see
> The distant scene—one step enough for me.
>
> I was not ever thus, nor pray'd that thou
> Shouldst lead me on.
> I loved to choose and see my path; but now,
> Lead thou me on!
> I loved the garish day, and, spite of fears,
> Pride ruled my will.
> Remember not past years.
>
> So long thy pow'r hath blessed me, sure it still
> Will lead me on
> O'er moor and glen, o'er crag and torrent, till
> The night is gone.
> And with the morn those angel faces smile,
> Which I have loved long since,
> And lost awhile![1]

As we watch our children grow, we know that, at any stage of childhood, they are not finished yet; but neither are they finished once they become adults. Nor are they, or we, finished once we marry and take on new roles as husbands and wives; nor are we finished once we become parents; nor are we finished when we move into middle age and that rocky, redefining period psychiatry refers to as "midlife crisis"; nor are we finished when we become old, even if we've managed to attain a measure of wisdom along the way; nor are we finished when we die. Becoming is eternal and turns all of life into an ever-new and grand adventure!

So, the first part of the answer to the question "Who am I?" is that we are becoming. We can't fully understand yet what we are becoming, but there is one thing we can know for sure: We are becoming that which we already are. Erich Fromm describes this process in a discussion on the source of the human conscience.

> It is important to distinguish between an "authoritarian" and a "humanistic" ethics. An authoritarian conscience . . . is the voice of an internalized authority, such as parents, state, religion. . . . This type of conscience . . . guarantees that the person can be relied upon to act always according to the demands of his conscience; but it becomes dangerous when the authorities command evil things. . . .
>
> Quite different from the authoritarian . . . conscience is the "humanistic" . . . conscience. It is not the internalized voice of an authority whom we are eager to please and afraid of displeasing; it is the voice of our total personality expressing the demands of life and growth. "Good" for the humanistic conscience is all that furthers life; "evil" is all that arrests and strangles it. The humanistic conscience is the voice of our self which summons us back to ourselves, to *become* what we potentially are.[2]

The story of Paul the Apostle illustrates this principle. Saul was a Jew who vigorously persecuted Christians. He was cruel, vicious, and relentless—this seemed to be who Saul was. But on the road to Damascus, he met the Lord and was changed forever. He became Paul, the apostle, kind, gentle, believer in grace and reconciler of Gentile and Jew. The question is, which persona represents the truth about this man? Which was his essence? Which was his soul? What was he like in the premortal existence?

In most discussions we hear about Paul's conversion, it is assumed that Saul is the real person and Paul is the changed, converted one. This assumption raises some serious problems. If he was evil, why did God choose him? If Christ thrust conversion onto an unseeking Saul, what does that mean for the doctrine of agency? And if God was willing to grab Saul by the scruff of his neck and turn him into Paul, why didn't he do the same thing to other evil leaders, such as Hitler, Mafia bosses, or Saddam Hussein? Perhaps our basic assumption about Paul is wrong. Perhaps Paul was not the converted or changed Saul; perhaps Saul was the changed and corrupted Paul.

Surely we revealed something of ourselves to our Heavenly Father during the premortal existence. And always, there is the possibility that when we come to earth, the circumstances we find ourselves in will profoundly influence and alter who we were there and what we started out to be. The only plausible explanation for what happened to Saul on the road to Damascus is not that a truly evil man was changed into a truly good man; the only plausible explanation is that a false front was revealed and then stripped away. Paul was not blinded after his conversion; he was blind before. His confrontation with the Lord on the road to Damascus opened his eyes, revealing what had been there all along—a man of God.

So are we, many times, blind to who we truly are. We know the natural man so well. We focus on it and try to fight our natural and sometimes evil tendencies, and in so doing we lose sight of the real truth about who we are and who we are becoming. We need to change our basic assumptions about ourselves. We were first children of God. And we are becoming that which we already are—Gods to be. When we act from that assumption, we can focus on the light and goodness within ourselves and the light that leads us on. We become more conscious of, and more responsive to, our yearnings to be close to and act like God. Gradually, throughout eternity, the natural man falls away, and, like a snake shedding its skin, our truer selves come to light and move toward God.

As Meister Eckhart said:

> The seed of God is in us. Given an intelligent and hard-working farmer and a diligent field hand, it will thrive and grow up to God, whose seed it is; and accordingly its fruits will be God-nature. Pear seeds grow up into pear trees, nut seeds into nut trees, and God seed into God.[3]

Beginners All

The scriptures often admonish us to become like little children. There are many ways to interpret that admonition, but we would probably all agree that we are not to remain childish or naive. The interpretation that I have always preferred is that we are to remain open and teachable. Eastern religions say it another way, admonishing their followers to consider themselves as beginners throughout their lives. Like the idea of becoming, the idea of always beginning brings a kind of freedom. To be a beginner is to be free to make and admit mistakes. To be a beginner is to be free to start over with any aspect of our lives. To be a beginner is to be free to redefine ourselves whenever, however, and however often we might choose, for truly you and I are not the same people today that we were last year or even last week, and we will not be the same tomorrow as we are today. To be a beginner is to free ourselves from preconceptions, misconceptions, judgments, and expectations. To be a beginner is to remove ourselves from any ruts we may be in and to free ourselves from the chains of habit. We try to move into each new day empty and open, receptive to whatever new insights we might gain and whatever lessons we can learn.

I've never been able to be that open all the time, so to help myself, I like to play little mind games, my own version of "let's pretend." You might want to try some of these exercises. The next time you go to church on Sunday, go as if you've never been there before. Pretend you were raised a Hindu, for example. You've never before heard the talks or prayers or hymns you will hear today. You've never met the people before. You've never considered the ideas before. Open up! Go with no expectations, no preconceptions, no judgments, no resentments, and no fond memories. You'll hear things you've never noticed before, be surprised by what has become commonplace, and notice and want to befriend people whom you might have overlooked before.

Pretend to be new at old things. Try it the next time you go to the temple. Pretend you're going for the first time. Go without expectations, no questions needing to be answered, no ideas you have wondered about, no things that have helped you in the past. Go empty, just to see what it's like. You'll notice things you've never seen before.

Try it the next time you and your spouse go on a date. Pretend it's your first one. Ask the questions you would ask on a first date. What are your hobbies and interests? What is your favorite subject to read about? What do you like best about your job? Then ask those kinds of questions, but in the context of being married. What do you like best about being married? What do you admire most about each of our children? What do you worry about most? What did you do before you were married that you don't do now and that you miss the most?

Try it with your children. Pretend you're the babysitter and you've never met the kids before. What upsets you? Are you overlooking problems as a mom or dad that you would not tolerate in a neighbor's family? Those are the things you need to spend some time on next.

Try it with yourself. Today you are starting brand new. Just for today the calendar is wiped clean. There are no obligations or commitments. The bills are paid and there is no correspondence or phone calls to make. Think about what you would be like if your circumstances were different. Who would you be if you were single instead of married, or married instead of single? What would you do with your time if you had no children, if your job were different, or if you had no job. Is there some central part of you that would be unchanged if you were homeless or handicapped or of a different race or gender? We can never truly know the answers to these questions, but our imagination can take us far when we let it. Using our imaginations in this way can help us define the part of ourselves, our values and character traits, that we would want to remain strong and constant regardless of our circumstances.

And finally, do the beginner exercise with yourself in a different way. Keep your circumstances the way they presently are but approach the tasks and obligations of the day as if you were doing each thing for the first time. Free yourself to create new routines and new patterns to your doing. Look at all you have to do as if you've never set priorities before. Would you prioritize your tasks differently? Or would you do things in the same way but see new meaning in each task?

Self-Development

If we are all children of God and are all trying to become like God, what does that mean for individuality? What role does choice play when I am trying to become like God? Are we all going after the same thing, all becoming the same persona? Of course not. We all have different talents and abilities, different interests, and different ways of perceiving ourselves, the world, and even the gospel. We each emphasize different things, respond to different things, and respond to the same things in different ways. That is a major reason why "child of God" is not a sufficient answer to the question "Who am I?" Our "becoming" throughout life is not just becoming like our Heavenly Father. Indeed, it implies our becoming, as fully as we can, who we most truly are as personalities; becoming truer and truer to our own best selves. This implies great effort, painfully honest introspection, and commitment to personal development.

When we think about personal development, a few things immediately come to mind: identifying and developing talents, keeping physically fit through exercise and good nutrition, and keeping spiritually fit through regular scripture study. All of these further our personal development. However, if we look closer, we realize much more is involved in personal development than these "to do" types of things. We often have problems with our own development because we get caught up in role-playing and become confused about who we really are. This goes right back to the question "Who am I?" Often we just don't know.

There are many reasons we don't know. One reason is that we are not conditioned or taught to know. From earliest childhood we are taught to conform, to obey the rules, and to live up to the expectations of others. In school we follow a prescribed curriculum outlined by others, and we are most successful when we answer teachers with what they want to hear. We are seldom encouraged to think for ourselves, to question, or to challenge authority. At church it's the same story. The answers are known. Learn to repeat them and you'll be fine. At home it's not much different. We must live up to our parents' expectations.

Once we reach adulthood, we are expected to marry and have children, and our gender then defines who we are. A woman is a wife and mother, and she is expected to find total fulfillment in serving in that capacity. If she does not, we may feel that something is wrong with her. A man is the family provider and begins to be defined by his job. I am no longer John Greene. I am now Mr. Carpenter or Mr. Engineer. Since we're all raised to please others and comply with authority, we often lose the ability to hear our own voices. Frantically striving to please others, we forget what pleases us.

Try to remember what pleases you. Try to remember what you liked to do in high school and college. We often forget what pleases us, but if we are to become who we most truly are, and if we are to avoid getting lost along the way, we need to remember. It is not selfish to develop our talents or pursue our own interests occasionally. Heavenly Father would not have given us our individual talents and interests if he did not intend for us to use them.

When I was five or six years into child-rearing, I realized that I wasn't much fun anymore. All the fun outings, vacation ideas, and adventures were coming from my husband. I read a magazine article about how often women lose themselves in child-rearing (leading to the "empty nest" syndrome when children are grown). The article suggested remembering what you liked to do most when you were in high school. I have wonderful memories of Girl Scouts as a high-school student. As a matter of fact, most of the lullabies I sang to my children were camp songs. How could I have forgotten! Remembering helped me start again. I took more walks in the woods with my children, and I volunteered to be a Girl Scout leader in my daughter's troop. I had a wonderful time, had more to contribute to the family, and learned a valuable lesson: I learned the value of remembering. As the children got older and I had a little more free time, I remembered how much I enjoyed reading in high school and which types of books I liked best. I started reading again and soon was reading everything I could get my hands on. After a couple of years of voracious reading, I started writing this book. You never know where a little remembering might lead you.

Solitude can also help. It's hard to find time to be alone, especially the kind of time I'm thinking about here, but now and then life presents us with the opportunity: a husband's business trip, a wife's visit to her family, parents or roommates leaving town for a week. Have you ever noticed that we are sometimes different when we're living alone than we are when surrounded by family or friends? How do you do things differently when you're alone? Do you sleep later or get up earlier? Do you go to bed earlier or later? Do you listen to different kinds of music or watch different kinds of television programs when you're alone? Do you call a different set of friends when you're on your own? Do you eat differently, work differently, or think differently when you're alone than when surrounded by family and friends? The next time you have an opportunity to be alone for a few days, keep a journal and

note the ways in which you are different. If your different ways of
being seem positive to you, incorporate one or two of them into
your usual routine. If some of your different ways of being reveal a
weakness or a fault, you've gained insight into yourself. Set some
goals, talk to some friends, read a book, or ask the Lord for help to
begin overcoming the weakness or correcting the fault. The
insights you gain in this process may help solve relationship problems when the family is back together.

We need other times of solitude too. Regular, small times.
Daily times, if possible. We all need time to be alone with ourselves, to rest from the business of our days, to separate from others and reconnect with the reality of God. From experiences in
quiet, introspective times, times with the scriptures, or times of
prayer, we get back in touch with the central truth of who we are
in a way that goes beyond definition or description in words. We
reach out to touch God, he touches us, and we find our selfhood
nurtured and affirmed.

Howard Thurman wrote:

> There is no clear distinction between mind and
> spirit, but there is a quality of mind that is more than
> thought and the process of thought: this quality
> involves feelings and the wholeness in which the life
> of man has its being. . . . There is the rest of detach-
> ment and withdrawal when the spirit moves into the
> depths of the region of the Great Silence, where
> world weariness is washed away and blurred vision is
> once again prepared for the focus of the long view. . . .
> Here God speaks without words and the self listens
> without ears. Here at last, glimpses of the meaning
> . . . of one's own life are seen with all their striving.
> To accept this is one meaning of the good line, "Rest
> in the Lord . . . "[4]

To wash away world-weariness and rest in the Lord—what a
beautiful image! Why do we let ourselves get so busy we deny ourselves that experience? We must make time for ourselves alone

with God. We must make this time happen. Early in the morning. At lunchtime. At night after everyone's asleep. In the kitchen, office, car, or bedroom. Time and space for our spiritual devotions can and must be made. We must realize that when we neglect our own self-development, we are also damaging our relationships with our families and friends. Regardless of service we may be performing, we are withholding ourselves from God and his influence. We are pitchers, not fountains; we simply have nothing to offer without frequent trips to the well. Most of all let yourself enjoy the process; becoming who you most truly are, looking at each day brand new, and pursuing the whole, complex beauty of personal development. Then offer it all, the process and the product, to yourself, your family, and your God.

Chapter 3: Marriage

Go from me. Yet I feel that I shall stand
Henceforward in thy shadow. Nevermore
Alone upon the threshold of my door
Of individual life, I shall command
The uses of my soul, nor lift my hand
Serenely in the sunshine as before,
Without the sense of that which I forbore—
Thy touch upon the palm. The widest land
Doom takes to part us, leaves thy heart in mine
With pulses that beat double. What I do
And what I dream include thee, as the wine
Must taste of its own grapes. And when I sue
God for myself, He hears that name of thine,
And sees within my eyes the tears of two.

—ELIZABETH BARRETT BROWNING

AH, MARRIAGE. The young long for it; the already married aren't so sure. Marriage starts with falling in love. Romance, happiness, and high hopes fill our hearts. We marry, and then life sets in: bills need to be paid, babies cared for, work performed—like so much else in life, love becomes hard work. Also, like so much else in life, that hard work turns out to be to our benefit.

Have you ever wondered why marriage plays so important a role in the plan of salvation? Marriage is more than a good thing in Mormon theology; it is also a moral obligation. Why? The obvious answer is, of course, procreation. Marriage and family are the vehicle our Heavenly Father uses to bring his spirit children to earth. Still, since most of us will marry anyway, what would be the harm if a few people chose to remain single? Yet the prophets have clearly and emphatically spoken on this, teaching that if someone remains single by choice, that person's eternal salvation is jeopardized. Why? What's the big deal, anyway?

I believe the big deal is love—not the falling-in-love ecstasy where marriage begins, but the working-at-love, satisfying yet difficult, where marriage ends up.

Martin Luther stated that marriage is the school of love. John the Beloved wrote, "Beloved, let us love one another: for love is of God; and every one that loveth is born of God, and knoweth God. He that loveth not knoweth not God; for God is love." (1 John 4:7–8.)

Love is important, but we often find it difficult even to figure out what it is. Oh, we know the feeling all right; we know the ecstasy of falling in love, the joy when our children are born, the comfort we enjoy with our friends. But the working-at-love, the love we have to learn about, the love the Lord commands us to give—*that* love, we're not so sure of.

If marriage is the school of love, what is it about loving we are to learn? If love is hard work, what is the work we must do? I found answers to these questions in M. Scott Peck's *The Road Less Traveled*:

> I define love thus: The will to extend one's self for the purpose of nurturing one's own or another's spiritual growth. . . .
>
> . . . The act of extending one's limits implies effort. One extends one's limits only by exceeding them, and exceeding limits requires effort. When we love someone our love becomes demonstrable or real only through our exertion—through the fact that for that someone . . . we take an extra step or walk an extra mile. Love is not effortless. To the contrary, love is effortful.
>
> Finally, by use of the word "will" I have attempted to transcend the distinction between desire and

action. Desire is not necessarily translated into action.
... Everyone in our culture desires to some extent to
be loving, yet many are not in fact loving. I therefore
conclude that the desire to love is not itself love. Love
is as love does. Love is an act of will—namely, both
an intention and an action. Will also implies choice.
We do not have to love. We choose to love. No matter how much we may think we are loving, if we are
in fact not loving, it is because we have chosen not to
love and therefore do not love despite our good inten-
tions. On the other hand, whenever we do actually
exert ourselves in the cause of spiritual growth, it is
because we have chosen to do so. The choice to love
has been made.[1]

To truly love another requires self-discipline, sacrifice,
patience, hope, and faith. It requires putting aside our preoccupations to make space in our thoughts for the other person's
thoughts. It requires paying close attention, listening, sharing of
ourselves, and suffering together. It requires all of these things
daily, hourly, and at inconvenient times, year after year.

Marriage, more than any other relationship, teaches us about
three components of love: commitment, acceptance, and communication.

Commitment

I chose to discuss commitment first because it is the founda-
tion on which the other two components of love rest. When a
spouse is committed to the marriage, the other spouse can't help
but be aware of that commitment. Likewise, when the commitment of one or both spouses is weak or lacking, that lack of commitment becomes a major factor in inhibiting both acceptance
and communication, simply because acceptance and honest communication both contain an element of risk. It is difficult to be

honest and open in our communication, to express anger, dissatisfaction, or assertiveness, if we fear that those very expressions
could lead to the dissolution of our marriage.

Commitment in marriage is twofold. First, it includes commitment to the institution of marriage itself—commitment to
endure to the end, regardless of circumstances or problems that
come up along the way. As Leo Buscaglia's mother was fond of
saying, "Murder—maybe. Divorce—never!"

The second is the commitment to put into the marriage whatever it takes to make it a satisfying and meaningful relationship.
A good marriage requires hard work, compromise, goodwill, and
frequent, sometimes painful, struggle. Marriage is more often an
emotional wrestling match than it is candlelight and roses. That
isn't because couples just don't get along well; rather, it is because
of the very nature of the relationship. Marriage comes loaded
with issues that need to be worked through so the family can
function and the relationship thrive—issues such as the division
of family responsibilities, the identification and appropriate use
of each person's abilities, the management of financial resources,
dominance and submission, the degree of independence or dependence each person requires or is willing to allow the other, and
breaking down personal barriers to invite the other into our private thoughts and feelings. As Victor L. Brown, Jr., wrote:

> Intimacy must include an active commitment to
> those we claim to love. And to endure, intimacy must
> be part of an ongoing structure. Breaking through the
> barrier that guards close relationships takes major
> effort and energy. It is at once a simple yet difficult
> experience. It is partially based on the sheer duration
> of years together. Even more important is a respect for
> the partner's personality coupled with an intense per-
> sonal devotion to the marriage, a commitment of
> character.[2]

It is in marriage and the struggles we experience there that we
come to understand what commitment feels like—the determi-

nation and courage it imparts, the suffering we must sometimes endure, and the steadfastness we must have in the face of vacillating emotions.

Those are invaluable lessons. Emotions do vacillate, times do get tough, spouses do disappoint each other. Commitment keeps the ship of marriage on an even keel. As we learn the requirements of commitment in marriage, we are then better prepared to follow through on our commitments to the Lord. Although we sometimes don't want to admit it, emotional vacillation occurs also in our spiritual relationships. I have loved God, and I have hated God. I have stepped out in faith, and I have shrunk in fear. I have felt and born strong testimony, and I have felt confused and filled with doubts. I have felt the Spirit so strongly I was sure I could have reached out and touched God, and I have felt so lost and alone I wondered if God truly existed. I often thought I was alone in those feelings. I know now that they are common. I've seen surveys that indicate up to 70 percent of active Church members have gone through periods of doubt strong enough to call that doubt loss of testimony. Doubt has been reported as persisting anywhere from a few months to more than a decade. What keeps people active in the Church when they feel "out of it"? Commitment. What we learn of commitment in marriage helps us through trials of our faith, and what we learn of commitment during trials of our faith can help us endure hard times in our marriage. Indeed, trials of faith can cause trials in our marriage, and vice versa. Enduring these trials together and sharing our spouses' troubles both enrich the marriage and build testimony.

To demonstrate the value of commitment in marriage, even in a period of doubt, let us look at how a "crisis of faith" might be experienced in a strong, committed marriage. We'll start with an active LDS couple who were married in the temple. Over the years they have had children, worked hard, and fulfilled their Church obligations. Then something happens to one of them—adversity of some sort: illness, an accident, or a death in the family. It might be exposure to previously unknown information or ideas. It might be a "midlife crisis," with its attendant questioning of all the so-called givens in one's life. Whatever the cause, one partner is now questioning and filled with doubts. For that person all the "knowing" has disappeared from his or her testimony. If there is strong commitment and support in the marriage, this crisis of faith can be a time of tremendous growth and deep-felt sharing. The troubled partner can share all doubts, questions, anger, or resentment, even if that anger is directed toward God. The couple can then work through the problems together. The doubting partner can feel free to ask questions out loud and to seek answers from his or her partner. He or she can also feel free to seek help from the bishop or a professional counselor because nothing is being hidden. As the problems are worked through, as questions are asked and answers found, one thing remains constant—the couple's commitment to each other and to the marriage. If one spouse's faith remains sure, as is usually the case, through his or her support and compassion, the troubled spouse feels free to share his or her burdens, his or her doubts. In the fasting, prayers, study, and suffering of the "sure" spouse, God "hears that name of thine, and sees within my eyes the tears of two," as Elizabeth Barrett Browning put it. When the crisis is over and testimony is regained, imagine the couple's joy and gratitude at having successfully weathered such a storm.

I have seen this scenario played out in the lives of several of my friends. Our former bishop was totally inactive in the Church for more than a decade. He was busy, successful, and brilliant. His career was too important to him to allow time to be given to the Church, and his faith was too simplistic to satisfy his mind. However, those ten years of inactivity were terribly difficult for his wife. Still, because of her commitment to her husband and their marriage, she had the strength to do the spiritual work of two. She remained fully active, taught their children, and offered many prayers on her husband's behalf. Since reentering Church activity, her husband has been bishop of two large wards. She is immensely proud of what he has both overcome and become, and he is grateful for her faithful prayers that helped him back. They both learned a great deal about commitment and love through their experience together.

Acceptance

Bishops and parents commonly counsel young people who are about to marry to take time the first few years to really get to know each other. Young people are told that they don't really know each other until after they have lived together awhile. People often forget, however, that this is true not only at the beginning of marriage but also throughout a couple's life together. Why? People change. Sometimes people change dramatically. Interests and hobbies change. Perspective, understanding, and abilities all change over the years. We must continue getting to know each other (which means communicating with each other). As we do, there must be an atmosphere of acceptance. Each spouse must allow the other to do his or her own becoming.

Heavenly Father recognizes and respects each individual's personality. He leads us each in different ways at different times. He challenges us each in different ways. He chastens us each in different ways. He teaches us each in different ways. Each spouse needs to allow the other to discover and develop his or her own personal relationship with God. Each spouse needs to allow the other to follow his or her own inner voice. Your Church callings won't be the same as your spouse's as you progress through life. Your "burning causes" probably won't be the same either. Your stumbling blocks, problems, and personal crises won't always be the same. All of these things are shared in marriage, but they cannot be dictated by one spouse to another. We cannot insist that because something is important to us, it must be of equal importance to our partner. Likewise, if something is important to our partner but seems rather unimportant to us, we can neither make the issue our own nor dismiss it as insignificant. Rather, we can respect the issue and its importance to our partner, offer our

interest and support, and reserve our best efforts and greatest
energy for our own issues.

Heavenly Father's most precious gift is our agency. Agency is
the bedrock principle on which the entire plan of salvation is
based. Acceptance of one's partner within the marriage relationship establishes an atmosphere in which each person is free to be.
Spiritual growth requires following the promptings of the Spirit.
It is hard to follow the light if your spouse feels threatened and
keeps trying to blow it out!

On the other hand, personal freedom is bound by limits.
Sometimes personal interests, desires, doubts, or drives must be
curtailed for the good of the family. Sometimes one partner must
act as a dam to the other's doubts, fears, or desires if, acting out
of deep moral conviction, that partner sees the other as driving
himself or herself into danger. I think of the tragic story Carol
Lynn Pearson recounts in *Goodbye—I Love You*. The book is the
story of Sister Pearson's marriage to a man who had homosexual
tendencies. After four children and many happy years, he left the
marriage to fully explore homosexuality. He moved to San
Francisco and had numerous affairs but could never find a partner with whom he could share his soul in the way he had with his
wife. Eventually he contracted AIDS and came back home,
where Sister Pearson nursed him until his death. This example is
an extreme one, and homosexuality is a complex issue—one I do
not pretend to understand. The point is, there are boundaries to
our freedom—which we cross at our peril. Marriage itself creates
boundaries and, from time to time, each partner may exert pres-
sure on the other to remain within those bounds.

In his book *Freedom and Destiny*, Rollo May uses the analogy
of a river to describe the relationship between freedom and destiny. The flow of the river represents personal freedom, the banks
of the river represent personal destiny—the limits of one's freedom. Without the banks, the river overflows, is dissipated, and
disappears into the sand. Flowing within the confines of its banks,
the river has direction, force, and vitality. So it is in marriage.
The marriage becomes part of one's destiny and imposes certain

limits on personal freedom. Within those limits, each partner works out his or her own personal and spiritual growth. There must be acceptance, allowance, and freedom, but these must be balanced with limits, consideration for others, and sacrifice for the common good. Thus the couple grows together, sometimes in different ways or at different times, or even in different directions, but with one another's support and within agreed-upon limits and boundaries.

Communication

Commitment is the head of a marriage—the reasoning, choice-making, conscious mind that keeps marriage stable and moving forward. Commitment is great glue. Acceptance is the heart of marriage: the trust, confidence, and affection that rejoices in the partners' individual personalities and recognizes individual needs and desires. Communication is the door that opens from the mind to the heart and back again.

So entwined are these three attributes of a growing marriage that they become difficult to separate. The strengthening of the relationship outlined in the "crisis of faith" example depends on the troubled partner's communicating doubts and questions to his or her spouse. Earlier I pointed out that people change. It is important for us to allow our partner (and ourselves, too) the freedom to change. As we change and grow, it is important to talk to each other. If we don't, we may find that eventually we no longer know each other.

Yet even in the best of marriages, talking freely can be difficult. Think about the way you talk to your best friend. With our best friends we can say almost anything; the words just spill out. This free, open communication can be difficult in marriage because marriage is such an emotionally charged relationship. The love is more intense, the desire to please is more intense, the disappointment is more intense, the hate is more intense, and the expectations are higher than in any other relationship. Honest talk within marriage can be scary.

Communication is difficult in marriage because the marriage relationship is loaded with the issues I mentioned earlier: the division of family responsibilities, the identification and use of individual abilities, the management of finances, dominance and submission, independence and dependence. These issues are not present in the same degree outside the family. These are thorny issues. I repeat, honest talk within marriage can be scary.

Yet talk we must. We must be sufficiently committed to the quality of the relationship to take the risk. We must also offer one another enough acceptance to minimize the risk. The talking and sharing that occur in a good marriage, like everything else discussed in this book, contain a spiritual element. The ability to think and talk, the development and use of language, is unique to human beings. We can understand the power of words when we read the word of God or hear a good sacrament meeting talk. Language, spirituality, and morality are all closely linked. The connection is amusingly but powerfully described by William Faulkner:

> When the last ding-dong of doom has clanged
> and faded from the last worthless rock hanging tide-
> less in the last red and dying evening, . . . even then
> there will still be one more sound: that of [man's]
> puny inexhaustible voice, still talking . . . not because
> he alone among creatures has an inexhaustible voice,
> but because he has a soul, a spirit capable of compas-
> sion and sacrifice and endurance.[3]

Man keeps on talking, man longs to talk, not just because man has a voice and language but because man has a soul. The spirit and the body, the soul of man, longs to share itself with another. That longing results in and is met and satisfied by marriage. But the longing to share is met and often satisfied only when the sharing continues, and the sharing can continue only when partners make a concerted effort to keep communication open, honest, and free-flowing. Communicating feelings and thoughts creates and enhances intimacy. Locking feelings up within ourselves creates alienation and isolation—but often we do it anyway. To some extent, even the most verbal and open couple will withhold feelings from one another, and most of us do it to an extent that harms the relationship at some time or another. That is quite natural. Victor L. Brown, Jr., speaks of the "barriers that guard human relationships."[4] We all have those barriers. One of marriages greatest challenges is to balance necessary respect for one's own and one's partner's barriers with the necessary breaking through of personal barriers so that intimacy may occur. To break through the barriers, we must confront a powerful force—the force of silence.

Silence can be wonderful, and many of marriage's special and intimate moments are accompanied by silence. That is not the kind of silence to which I am referring. The silence that is destructive to human relationships is the silence that accompanies fear, denial, anger, and hurt.

Denial is the response that many of us mere mortals give to significant problems that arise in our lives. We pretend problems don't exist in the hope they will go away or solve themselves. Silence protects our pretense. As long as we don't talk about the problems, we can go on pretending all is well. To break the silence that accompanies denial requires tremendous courage and a willingness to face the very problems we have been avoiding in the past. In those cases, the process of breaking silence is nothing more or less than communal repentance. The first steps in this repentance are recognition of the problem and confession. As with personal repentance, the first steps are the hardest.

Fear in the context of close family relationships is, in reality, the anxiety that accompanies allowing ourselves to be vulnerable. Communication can break through the barriers that guard all close relationships. Those barriers are the psychic boundaries we put up to protect ourselves. Open, close communication pierces the barriers, requiring us to "drop our guard." And to "drop our guard" is to become and feel vulnerable. We expose our tenderness, risking rejection or hurt; we expose our anxieties, revealing that we are often less than confident; we expose our anger and dissatisfaction, risking damage to the relationship. Afraid of such exposure, we often retreat into silence.

To take the risk, to break the silence, to begin the conversation—these take effort, courage, and self-discipline. Here again is the work of love, the extending of oneself for the sake of another. The risk we are taking—the risk of rejection or disappointment—feels like nothing less than offering our hearts to be broken. But wasn't that the message of the Savior's life; from his first sermon to his death on the cross, he offered his heart to be broken. Marriage is a lifelong opportunity for us to offer our hearts to another—even if it means occasionally having them broken. We offer our hearts in many ways—in small acts of kindness, consideration, and respect—but none is so great as the offering we make in communication: listening with full attention and empathy, talking with true and honest feeling, sharing with each other the good, the bad, and the ugly. Talk and listen; talk of doubts, talk of fears, talk of tenderness, talk of anger, talk of embarrassments, talk of accomplishments, talk of disappointments, talk of joy, talk of remorse, talk of hopes and dreams. As partners in marriage, we need to offer our hearts to one another. As we do, our barriers will melt and our hearts will soften, and a soft heart is fertile ground for the Spirit of God.

Chapter 4: Parenting

Lo, children are an heritage of the Lord: and the fruit of the womb is his reward. As arrows are in the hand of a mighty man; so are children of the youth. Happy is the man that hath his quiver full of them.

—PSALM 127:3–5

CHILDREN ARE A WONDERFUL PARADOX. We are eager to have them. We readily admit they make life more enjoyable and satisfying. Expectant couples are afloat, and babies bring smiles to everyone's faces.

But then there's the other side. Infants and toddlers are so demanding! They take so much time! Their care often leaves parents exhausted and gives marriage its greatest test. As fatigue takes its toll, new mothers feel all used up. "Why doesn't he help more? Why do I have to do so much?" New fathers feel neglected and ignored. "Hey, I'm still part of this family! Don't I count anymore?" Adding to the problem, we begin to slip in our spiritual pursuits. Scripture study, prayer, even family night often get only sporadic attention. Sacrament meeting becomes a trial. It seems just when we need the Spirit the most, it becomes the hardest to obtain. Why? What purpose does that serve, and why is raising children so important that all who can are commanded to bear them?

At a time when we need the Spirit so much, why don't we feel it more often? Why can't we have "temple feelings" every day? I suspect we're not supposed to. I suspect that being close to the Lord in that sense is not what we are here for. In fact, being with the Lord is what we left behind. We left him behind to see how we might do on our own. Moreover, we were commanded to multiply and replenish the earth that we might have joy in our posterity. But joy is not the only thing our posterity brings us. It also brings experience, learning, understanding, patience, and selflessness. In short, raising children propels us in our quest for greater spiritual maturity.

What Is a Child?

What is a human being?

What are you and I?

Latter-day Saints are quite familiar with these age-old questions. In an attempt to answer them, let's go back to the *very* beginning.

Hugh Nibley wrote of this time: "Who are we? Abraham sees that as the ultimate question and meets it handily: intelligence . . . , beyond which nothing is to be said. You can doubt everything else, but that much you must grant—there were those intelligences, because they still are. What the book of Abraham tells me is that, if this moment of consciousness is real, then it is all real. I can bear unshakable testimony to one thing: I am here."[1]

Look into a baby's eyes, and what do you see looking back? Consciousness, awareness, alertness, intelligence—teaching you about your own nature any time you choose to learn. Watch your nine-month-old, two-year-old, four-year-old, and even fourteen-year-old. To children, the whole world is a magnificent university, and children pursue learning with incredible gusto and insatiable curiosity. Children *must* learn. Children *must* explore. Children *must* grow. These things are the very essence of their natures. Learning and growing are the essence of our human nature as well, our very raison d'être. Sometimes we forget; often we forget. As adult responsibilities and obligations press upon us, we lose sight. Making a living, maintaining the home, caring for the children, filling the calling—these things preoccupy us so we often miss the point. Reaching the goal and completing the task become the important thing. Our minds are so occupied with the end point, we forget that the point of doing is learning. We forget to pay attention as we go. Proverbs admonishes us: "With all thy getting get understanding." (Proverbs 4:7.)

Watching our children eagerly going after understanding; seeing their bright, eager faces; hearing their endless, seeking questions; looking and searching for answers with them—all these remind us.

As our children get older, the questions don't stop; they just become more difficult, and hence more helpful to our own growth. Discussing difficult issues such as racism, economic inequality, war, peace, nationalism, science, religion, and so on, can help us remember and more clearly define our own values and priorities. We revisit our own adolescent questions with greater maturity and are often surprised to find we now have answers. We also rediscover the joy of struggling with a thoughtful question.

Awareness—alertness—intelligence. Raising children can put us back in touch with that central core of who we are.

Seeing Is Believing

One part of intelligence is understanding; the other part is awe. As children pursue understanding with gusto and curiosity, their discoveries fill them with a sense of wonder. I remember a friend of mine having the following conversation with her two-year-old on the way into her house after an evening meeting.

Mom: "Look Nathan, there's the moon."

Nathan, wide-eyed and open-mouthed: "Oh. Is it, Mom? Oh."

Then both stood in the driveway, gazing up together.

We've all had such experiences with our children, and the experience is not limited to just young children. Ask any Scoutmaster or adviser from girl's camp. Remember the times yourself. Sometimes the kids point out the wonder; sometimes, because we're with them and we want them to notice, we do. But always and frequently our children bring us face-to-face with wonder and awe.

Just yesterday I was walking to the bus stop with my five-year-old. We live in New England, and it is autumn. Yesterday it rained, and most of the leaves that were overhead are now underfoot. As she ran down the sidewalk, my delighted daughter scooped up an armful of leaves, threw them in the air, and exclaimed, "Look, Mommy, it's a gold mine!" I wanted to scoop her up and throw *her* in the air shouting, "Look, Lord, it's a gold mine!" After she got on the bus and I was walking home alone, I scooped up my own handful of leaves and threw them in the air, twirling around in delight.

Parents delight in their children's delight with the natural world. Trees, grass, rivers, lakes, dirt, worms, moths, butterflies, stars, moon, and sky all become new and wonderful again as we reexperience them through our children's wide-open, so-alert eyes. The wonder continues as our children grow and have first after first—biking, roller skating, games and sports, buses, computers, friendships, reading, television, blossoming sexuality, cars, increasing sensitivity to others, new testimonies, first temple visits, and missions. All become expressions of the miraculous world in which we live and the marvelous complexities of the human body, mind, heart, and soul—Heavenly Father's most precious creation. As Shakespeare wrote, "O wonderful, wonderful and yet again wonderful."[2]

No Pain, No Gain

I'd love to go on about the delightful ways in which children teach us, but there are other, less delightful ways, and they are no less important.

I believe that these *less* delightful ways are all tied up with what philosophers refer to as the "human condition." The "human condition" is a complex combination of human attributes that the scriptures call "the natural man." It is partly our separation from one another, our inability to truly know one another's experiences, our inability to ever really walk in another's shoes. Add to that isolation a healthy dose of self-interest and self-absorption, season heavily with pride and laziness, and you have the "human condition!" In parenting, it goes something like this.

We enter parenting thinking we are the center of the child's universe. We prepare ourselves to be a good center, reading the right books on pregnancy, delivery, breast feeding, and child development. We learn how important *we* are to our children. We learn how important the environment *we* create is. We learn how important it is to set a good example and teach our children. Sometimes we get so carried away with our own importance that we totally discount what our children bring with them into the world!

Last year we had a Relief Society lesson on the importance of teaching our children well. The lesson was good. However, I found the resulting discussion a bit disturbing. One woman referred to our children's minds as blank slates on which our teachings are written. Another referred to our children as empty computers and parents as the programmers. That's a lot of responsibility. Oh my, no. Oh my, not true.

At least not totally true. We *are* important, of course. We *do* need to be responsive, caring, teaching, supportive, and at least fairly consistent. In fact, in many ways, parents *are* the center of their children's universe. However, in many ways, we are not. We often spend our lives learning, somewhat painfully, the ways in which we are not. For children are also subject to the "human condition," and the real center of the child's universe is the child, just as the center of my universe is me and the center of your universe is you. That isolation and self-centeredness presents one of the major spiritual tasks of life on this earth—learning to move beyond ourselves. Moving beyond ourselves is something we work on, struggle with, and overcome in bits, spurts, and wonderful occasions, throughout our lives. Parenting not only gives us the opportunity to work on that problem; it also focuses our attention on it, badgers us about it, beats us up and helps us come to terms with it over and over again. Here are some examples of how that happens.

As the parents of young children, we are proud as peacocks. Eagerly we exchange tales with other young parents: he's walking at only nine months old; she's dressed up in the most adorable clothes at church; he's precocious at the piano; she's a straight-A student; and on it goes. These feelings are universal and, believe it or not, they can be detrimental to you and your children. No one likes to be someone else's prize on display.

Children as an annex or accomplishment—taking credit, taking blame. We all do it. Our kid's accomplishments make us proud. Our kid's difficulties make us embarrassed. Both are seen as a reflection on *us*.

What are some of the fruits of taking credit and taking blame? Parents often compete with each other, using their children's accomplishments as evidence of their own worth. Parents often judge one another if children seem to be having problems. Peer support can disappear just when it is needed the most.

What happens to the children in this scenario? They may become self-conscious and uncomfortable. Children often become resentful of their parents, sensing that being shown off is not what they are for. If children are slow in their development or have problems, the parents' discomfort simply exacerbates the problem. Young children who are compared to other children, even if the comparison is favorable, become fearful of making mistakes or of not continuing their high level of performance.

This whole discussion may have you squirming. It had me squirming as I wrote it—not because I recognized myself and felt bad, though I did, but because I wasn't sure of what I was saying or feeling. It's natural to take pride in our children. It seems to be a positive part of parenting. Yet I've seen the destructive part as well. To clarify my own thinking, I had to come up with a second word, a word that encompasses the positive aspects of parental pride while leaving the possessive part out. The word I found is *regard*.

Regard: To observe attentively. To think highly
of; esteem; respect; consideration; concern.

Let's look at the difference between pride and regard. Through
the ages, pride has been designated as sinful. President Ezra Taft
Benson indicated that pride is the universal sin and is often very
destructive. The pride we feel in our children is no different.
Why? Because pride is a self-directed emotion. Pride says: "Look
at me. Look at what I've done." When we take pride in our children, we take credit away from them for ourselves.

Regard describes quite a different set of emotions. Holding a
child in high regard is child-centered. It is a quiet, respectful emotion. It is not dependent on a child's accomplishments or threatened by a child's weaknesses or mistakes. Regard signifies
acceptance and recognizes each person's essential value. It takes
neither credit nor blame. Regard says: "I accept you as you are. I
value you as you are. I cherish you because you are, not because
you do, simply because you are. I do not take credit for your success nor blame for your failure. Your success or failure does not
enhance or diminish my esteem for you. You are a child of God
and a child of mine, and I love you." That does not mean we do
not suffer with our children when they fail or rejoice with them
when they succeed. But it keeps their failure or success as theirs.

For most of us, the emotions we feel toward our children contain both pride and regard. Our task is to minimize the pride and
maximize the regard. As we do, we might expect to see different
results. First of all, we might feel freer—freer to allow our children to be who they already are rather than who we might want
them to be, freer to accept our own shortcomings as parents, freer
from the tendency to judge others, and freer to grow together
with our children. As pride is replaced with the acceptance of
regard, fear and anxiety decrease while trust and faith increase—
trust in God, trust in life, trust in ourselves, and trust in our children. The exchange of pride for regard might sound like this:
"Yes, my son is walking now. Yes, he's already twenty months old.
Isn't it wonderful the way human beings unfold!"

With regard, we can behold our children's development much as Nathan beheld the moon—with wonder and awe. Gone is the ego involvement, the comparing, the pushing; in their place is acceptance—of ourselves, our children, and the whole process of growth that life puts us through. We become more objective about our children's successes and less threatened by their mistakes, failures, and even sins. We are sinners ourselves. We strive not to be, while we accept that we are. So are they. Now parent and child can be free to grow closer to the Lord together.

As Polly Berrien Berend wrote:

> Like wheat and tares these two ideas grow up together. Sometimes we march in all heavy-footed, trying to yank out the weeds, trampling the wheat, and only breaking off the tops of the weeds and sowing their seeds. Other times we stand back. Then we see that the wheat is strong and true and that the weeds will die out as the wheat grows. In this beholding we understand ever more clearly our own confusion. *We even notice that whatever is governing us is also governing our children.* . . . As the years go by we find ourselves telling them less and learning more from them. We also see that they learn better from our learning than they ever did from our telling.[3]

Waiting on the Lord

Another important way raising children moves us along is by helping us realize our dependence on the Lord. Parenting is such a complex task and dealing with children can be so difficult and perplexing that we are sometimes left feeling helpless and confused. Feeling helpless and confused can lead to our turning to the Lord for help. That in itself is progress; moreover, the answers that come often help *us* even more than they do our children. Here are two illustrations from my own experience.

Most parents have had to deal with a child's temper tantrums. I remember one tantrum in particular. The child was four. I don't remember how his tantrum started. I do remember feeling helpless—helpless to fix things for him and helpless to calm him down. I said a silent prayer: "What should I say? What can I do?" The answer came immediately: "Just listen." I did. I looked into my angry son's eyes with concern and just listened. He shouted and screamed and yelled and stamped his feet as I nodded my head in sympathy. Then he stopped, gave a "so there" nod of his head, turned, and left the room. The tantrum was over. He was calmed down, even seemed to feel understood, and I hadn't said a word! Not one word.

A year or so later, I had a similar experience with my twelve-year-old son who had just been introduced to what he perceived as the agony of Saturday night general priesthood meetings. After the first one, he announced that he hated it and would never go again! Well, time marches on, and soon it was time for another priesthood meeting telecast from Salt Lake City. For several days before the meeting, our son let it be known he was *not* going, while my husband insisted he was. The dreaded day arrived, and my husband pulled the ultimate cop-out. He called from work to say he would be working late and would meet our son at church. I had to get him there! Aaahhh! I did not want a scene. I did not want a power struggle. I did not want my son to go to the meeting so upset he would gain nothing from it. I did want him to go.

He came home, walked in the door, looked at me, and promptly declared, "I'm not going! You can't make me!" I responded with a profound, "Oh." I went upstairs and prayed my parent prayer: "Lord, what do I do? What do I say?" The answer was the same (the Lord's parent answer, I presume): "Say as little as possible. Listen to your son." This time I was more skeptical. After all, this was no four-year-old I was dealing with! Nervously I went downstairs and sat next to him on the couch. We looked at each other.

Me: "You really don't want to go, do you?"

Son: "No! I hate those meetings!" (Silence. Long silence.)

Me: "I guess they can be pretty boring."

Son: "They're useless! You just sit and watch these old guys talk on TV. It's worse than history class in school!" (His face perked up.) "Does this mean I don't have to go?"

Me, gently: "No, you still have to go."

Son: "Oh. Well . . . I guess there will be other kids there. Maybe they'll have ice cream after. I'd better get ready."

He left, and I stayed on the couch—in shock! All I had to do was get out of his way, and he worked it out himself.

What have I learned from such experiences? I've learned that God answers prayers, and he answers truthfully. I've learned humility, the kind so beautifully described in a previous quotation: "They learn more from our learning than they ever did from our telling." And, perhaps most important, I've learned to trust the Lord, and I've learned to trust my children.

I think that last one is particularly difficult for parents. Standing back and letting our children find their own way can be so important and so frightening! Yet, during those times when the only assistance we can offer our children is our prayers, our faith will grow in leaps and bounds. I'd like to share one last experience I've had with my children. The experience continues to teach me about faith, for its final outcome is as yet unknown.

My oldest daughter is very bright. She particularly loves math and science. When she was seven, she announced she was going to be an astronaut when she grew up. What fun! We bought her books about space. We bought her a telescope. She went to space camp. We all had a wonderful time dreaming about her future in the stars. One evening when she was ten or eleven, I thought maybe I should temper her dreams with a little dose of reality. After all, she was very young, and people often abandon their childhood aspirations as they grow up. I wanted her to feel free to examine other options. I also wanted to be sure she wouldn't feel like she was disappointing us if her life took her in another direction. When she started talking about being an astronaut, I calmly said, "Well, you might not be an astronaut. You might change your mind."

"Oh, but Mother," she insisted, "I *am* going to be an astronaut!"

I wasn't going to argue the point, so I quickly agreed, and she went off to bed.

After the kids were all in bed that night, I took the chance to relax on the sofa. As I picked up a book, I glanced up at the family picture that hung over the fireplace. My eyes were immediately drawn to my daughter's face, and this thought intruded forcefully into my mind: "Mother, don't interfere with your daughter's destiny!"

I was dumbfounded! "Oh my," I thought. "She really is going to be an astronaut!"

I've pondered that experience many times in the ensuing years. I've shared it with my daughter, and we've discussed it. Neither one of us feels we have a testimony that she will someday be an astronaut and fly to the moon. Both of us feel we have a testimony of something far more precious than that. We have a testimony that she *has* a destiny, a mission in life that is totally between her and her Heavenly Father. It is, frankly, none of my concern. I don't know what it is, and my involvement in her finding it will be minimal. She doesn't know what it is either. Heavenly Father does, and he will guide her to it just as surely as he has guided me.

Trust him. Trust them. Teach them to trust themselves and follow their hearts.

I Love You

Perhaps the most significant thing children teach us is how love. In *The Road Less Traveled*, M. Scott Peck tells us that love the will to extend ourselves to promote our own or someone else spiritual growth. Isn't that what parenting is all about?

A wonderful illustration of how parenting can involve extend ing ourselves to promote our children's spiritual growth is found in Sherrie Johnson's *Spiritually Centered Motherhood*. Sister

Johnson starts her book describing the overwhelming joy she felt
at the birth of her first child. She also describes an overwhelming
sense of responsibility: "This precious firstborn grew and
Heavenly Father sent seven more daughters to our home. With
each my joy increased, but there also came an increase in my
overwhelming sense of responsibility to return these choice spirits, unblemished, to our Heavenly Father."[4]

Many parents feel these same emotions as their children are
born, but where love is concerned, emotion is not enough. Love
is as love does. Sister Johnson went much further:

> What steps did I need to take to develop spiritu-
> ality in my children? What was the first thing I should
> teach them, and the second and third? How should I
> go about teaching them?
>
> I still felt that the answers must be in the scrip-
> tures, but there was so much there I didn't know
> where to begin. I wanted a lesson plan or guide. Then
> one day, *after some months of study and prayer,* I was
> talking with a man about King Benjamin's great ser-
> mon in the Book of Mormon (Mosiah 2–5). As he
> told me about the steps he had found in the speech
> for personal conversion, firecrackers went off in my
> mind. "That's it!" I thought. "If King Benjamin could
> lift his people to the level of commitment he did in
> that one speech, how could my effectiveness be
> improved by using those same steps . . . with my chil-
> dren?"
>
> I went home and *prayerfully began to study the
> speech. I paraphrased each verse in my own words. I read
> it over and over again. Then, after many weeks of prayer
> and study . . .* [5]

Sister Johnson didn't stop at feeling responsible for her children. She didn't stop at wondering how she might promote their
spiritual growth. She didn't do a little here and a little there.
Sister Johnson agonized over her children. She questioned. She

struggled. She studied. She prayed. Finally, she succeeded. She worked out a program for teaching the gospel to her children. Then she implemented her plan. As she did these things, she did something else: she grew spiritually. She strengthened and improved her self-discipline, her testimony, her dedication, her commitment—her ability to love.

Sister Johnson's hard work in behalf of her children is not so unusual. We all do it. Sacrifice, hard work, chronic fatigue, worry, and pain are all part of every good parent's experiences. We just need to remember that the experiences are for our own benefit as well as our children's. Nowhere else is the motivation to extend ourselves more powerful and compelling than in our relationship with our children. Nowhere else is the opportunity to extend ourselves so ever-present.

I like the description of this process in *The Velveteen Rabbit,* by Margery Williams:

> "What is REAL?" asked the Rabbit one day. . . . "Does it mean having things that buzz inside you and a stick-out handle?"
>
> "Real isn't how you are made," said the Skin Horse. "It's a thing that happens to you. When a child loves you for a long, long time, not just to play with but REALLY loves you, then you become Real."
>
> "Does it hurt?" asked the Rabbit.
>
> "Sometimes," said the Skin Horse, for he was always truthful. "When you are Real you don't mind being hurt."
>
> "Does it happen all at once, like being wound up," he asked, "or bit by bit?"
>
> "It doesn't happen all at once," said the Skin Horse. "You become. It takes a long time. That's why it doesn't often happen to people who break easily, or have sharp edges, or who have to be carefully kept. Generally, by the time you are Real, most of your hair has been loved off, and your eyes drop out and you get

loose in the joints and very shabby. But these things
don't matter at all, because once you are Real you
can't be ugly, except to people who don't understand."[6]

Nowhere else are we so willing to become worn out and
shabby for the benefit of someone else as we are in parenting.
Nowhere else are the consequences of choosing not to do so as
painful or immediately apparent as they are in parenting.

Praise the Lord for our children! Praise the Lord for the motivation they give us to overcome our own laziness, put aside our
preoccupation and self-concern, and focus our attention on them!
Praise the Lord for the opportunity to attend to their needs, listen to them, see with their wonder-filled eyes, teach them, correct them, agonize with them, rejoice with them, and grow ever
closer to the Lord with them!

Chapter 5: Friendship

When all is done, a person of related mind, a brother or sister by nature, comes to us so softly and easily, so nearly and intimately, as if it were the blood in our proper veins, that we feel as if some one was gone, instead of another having come: we are utterly relieved and refreshed: it is a sort of joyful solitude. . . . But only that soul can be my friend, which I encounter on the line of my own march, that soul to which I do not decline, and which does not decline to me, but, native of the same celestial latitude, repeats in its own all my experience.

—RALPH WALDO EMERSON

LAST WEEK I MET a friend for lunch. That is something I don't do often, for, like you, I am busy and have trouble finding time for such an indulgence. But last week I met a friend for lunch. I drove to her house, walked in, and instantly felt at home. We had a nice lunch and talked for over two hours. It was hard to leave, but when I did I felt refreshed and renewed. I thought of how easy it was for us to talk and how open and comfortable we were with each other. Friendships are unique relationships. They are different from relationships within the family. We can learn much from those differences. We can learn about ourselves, our family relationships, our relationship with the Savior, and, again, the nature of love.

Friendship and Choice

The first unique component of friendship is that, throughout the time the friendship lasts, it is voluntary. Friendships are free of strings. There are no vows, no "for better or for worse" as in marriage, and no "you take what you get" as in parenting. We choose our friends and, if the relationship no longer fits, we let it die and move on to other friends. Because of that, friendship is often the arena in which we both feel and offer the greatest acceptance. We do not set out to change a friend, and our friends seldom attempt to change us. Our best friends are often our best friends because to them, and them alone, we can say anything. It is with our friends that we share fears or frustrations that are too large and threatening or too small and petty to discuss with anyone else.

Emerson wrote: "A friend is a person with whom I may be sincere. Before him, I may think aloud. I am arrived at last in the presence of a man [or woman] so real and equal that I may drop even those undermost garments of dissimulation, courtesy, and second thought, which men never put off, and may deal with him with the simplicity and wholeness, with which one chemical atom meets another."[1]

Our unguarded, spontaneous conversations with friends provide spiritual renewal. Through these conversations, friends "bear one another's burdens." Shared problems are always easier to deal with, and the exchange of emotional support is the kind of service that is at the heart of living the gospel. Our friends can give us an objective view of our problems. Comments and responses to shared secrets often lend insight we would be hard pressed to gain on our own. We, in turn, can often offer similar insights to our friends. Open-hearted conversations with friends are a wonderful sounding board. Sometimes our worries or complaints are petty or silly. Sensing this, we are reluctant to voice them to a spouse or authority figure such as a parent, bishop, or even professional counselor. Nonetheless, these concerns bother us, and the more we think about them, the larger they become. Ah, but we can say anything to our best friends, and so we do. Often, as we do, our problems melt away, for petty worries or complaints are often dispelled the moment they are spoken out loud. Friends provide a great service to each other just by being there, listening without judgment.

Moreover, conversations with friends often go far beyond everyday concerns and problems, great or small. In searching conversations with our dearest friends, we can explore the infinite, question the unquestionable, and glimpse the unknowable. Deep conversations of that type help us sort out who we are, what we believe, and what we cherish.

I recently had such a conversation with a dear friend. This friend is a member of our ward but is on assignment to a dependent branch, so I don't see him often. He has a wonderful intellect and great spiritual sensitivity. On the rare occasions I do see him, I seek him out in hopes of having the kind of conversation we enjoyed last week. We began discussing common experiences as seminary teachers, including questions teenagers often ask. We then discussed one of those questions: "If God created the universe, who created God?" We were immediately engrossed in a lively discussion that soon attracted other members of the group—we all hunger for such discussions. It was great fun. It was lively and stimulating. But it was far more than just stimulating fun. I thought I had some answers to that age-old question. He challenged those answers. He proposed an idea I hadn't considered before, but one I will be considering for some time to come. And he said some things I rebelled against, rejected, found disturbing—yet I couldn't say why. I thought about our conversation for several hours after our meeting. I compared what he had to say with my own experiences. I figured out what I didn't like and why. As I did that, I identified and reaffirmed my own most cherished beliefs about the nature of God. In such conversations, friends hold up a mirror to our minds, helping us clarify our own thoughts and interpret our own experiences.

We often fall prey to the belief that the only kind of spiritual pursuits are church attendance, scripture study, and prayer. These are important. Had I not spent solitary time in study and prayer, I would have had nothing to say to my friend. The conversation would not have happened. But the conversation itself was a spiritual pursuit every bit as important as my own personal study. Through that conversation, I was given access to someone else's scripture study and prayer, someone else's insights and understanding, someone else's holy space.

Friendship and Renewal

Friends help us evaluate and renew ourselves through conversations and shared experiences as described above. They help us renew ourselves in other ways as well. Human beings change. Change can be difficult, and friends can help. Friendships bring a new element to personal change. They do so because friendships change. Friends change. We are making new friends throughout our lives. Samuel Johnson said, "If a man does not make new acquaintances as he advances through life, he will soon find himself alone." We are aware of that at some level, so we are constantly making new friends. New people are constantly moving into our neighborhoods, communities, and wards. We acquaint ourselves with these people and often choose a few to befriend. So? What does that have to do with personal change? To answer that question, let's look at some examples of personal change and the impact people around us have on our efforts to change.

We have an unusual bishopric in our ward. All three of the men spent an extended period of their adult lives in inactivity. All of them admit that coming back to full activity in the Church was difficult.

Coming back is always humbling. Everyone in the ward knows you have had problems with the gospel. You might be treated with extra enthusiasm and warmth, or you might be treated with aloofness, but either way, you are treated differently. Because of that, it is hard to feel comfortable with the "new you." The change feels false, like a garment you can put on and take off but is not a permanent part of you. Gradually new people move into the ward and become friends. Incoming new people have no knowledge of prior inactivity, at least no first-hand knowledge. With these new friends, your activity and testimony are assumed.

Gradually the new behavior no longer feels new; the change becomes easier to integrate into your self-image and becomes part of you. Part of this process is simply a function of time, but it can be greatly facilitated as new friends enter our lives.

I experienced this for myself when I began to write. When I moved into my present ward, I was the quintessential "Mormon Mom" with a three-year-old, a two-year-old, and six-month-old twins. For many years I filled that role, adding two more children along the way. I was busy with the usual things and served in the usual ways. I enjoyed listening to the more "intellectual" members of the ward discuss the finer points of scripture or doctrine, but I rarely participated.

Five years ago, I went back to work part-time. Because I worked night shifts, I found work held a wonderful fringe benefit—an occasional hour or two to read. I rekindled my lost love for reading and, after a couple of years of reading and thinking, I began to write. Writing clarified and focused my thinking, and I began to change. I became more outgoing at church. I participated in class discussions more. Often my comments were related to my writing and were, therefore, fairly well thought out. Old friends often looked at me with a little surprise in their eyes, and I felt embarrassed and uncomfortable. "Just who do you think you are?" was a phrase that popped into my mind with disturbing regularity. "What makes you think you can write a book?" was another one.

Then I made a new friend. She was new in the ward and was a bright, articulate woman. She was called to be our spiritual living leader, and she gave wonderful lessons that never failed to surprise and delight me. Sometimes I would make a comment in her class that seemed to surprise and delight her. We became friends. The changes I have made in myself don't feel awkward or uncomfortable when I am with her. The new me is the only me she has ever known. She assumes that the new me is the real me. She assumes that writing a book is a perfectly natural thing for a person like me to do. Now when self-doubt raises its head, when questions pop into my mind, I talk to my new friend and come away reaffirmed and reassured. For me, the message is that if I want to make some significant changes in my life, I must first do some work to make the changes start, then find a new friend to make the changes stick.

As Anaïs Nin wrote, "Each friend represents a world in us, a world possibly not born until they arrive, and it is only by this meeting that a new world is born."[2]

We Have So Much in Common

The second unique element of friendship is commonality. We are a different sex than our spouse. We are a different generation than our children. Not so friends. The majority of our friends are of the same sex and of similar age and life experiences. Friends can offer one another a depth of understanding and empathy that can be hard to find within the family. Your wife may not understand the pressures you are under at work, but your friends there do. Your husband may not understand your frustrations with several preschoolers underfoot, but your neighbors do. To be understood, to understand another, these are not small things. If nothing else, the experience of being understood teaches us something of its value, which can help us work harder at offering understanding to others. If nothing else, offering understanding to someone who is easy for us to understand gives us experience we can use when the process is more difficult.

There are other benefits. Because friends have so much in common and because they offer such total acceptance to each other, friends often develop a deep trust in one another. Indeed, trust and confidence are often the first elements of friendship and a basic requirement before an acquaintance turns into a real friend.

I had an interesting experience with this kind of trust several years ago. An acquaintance of mine from our ward was having serious difficulties in her marriage. She needed someone to talk to. There were several women in the ward that she felt comfortable with and to whom she felt she could freely talk. However, she didn't feel she could trust any of these women to keep a confidence. During preceding years, each of these women had told her stories about others that should have been kept confidential. I was her visiting teacher at the time, so she thought she might be able to talk to me. But first she wanted to test me. Over a period of six months, she shared a few things with me that she felt would not be too damaging or embarrassing if they were spread around the ward. Then she waited. She waited for someone else to repeat the story. She waited for someone else to come up to her and say, "I'm sorry to hear you're having problems." Fortunately for both of us, I was smart enough to keep my mouth shut, so she waited in vain. When she was sure I would keep her confidence, she opened up. I was her confidante, counselor, and sounding board for three years as she and her husband struggled with their problems and finally divorced. Once her life was more settled and it was my turn to have problems, she was one of only two people I confided in and found comfort with. Our lives have gone separate ways in recent years, but whenever we chance to see each other, we can talk freely. I treasure her friendship, a friendship that would never have occurred had she found me untrustworthy.

Beyond Having So Much in Common

Our easiest, most comfortable friendships are formed with those with whom we have shared interests or experiences. Take a minute to review your own friendships. How many of your friends are older or younger than yourself? How many are in different economic circumstances or of a different race or religious background? For many of us, the answer to that question is "None." That is to be expected. However, it is not always for the best. The Lord has commanded us to love our enemies, and the gospel requires us to offer friendship to all our acquaintances. Here the Church truly comes to the rescue. I don't know if this is true in Utah, but in New England our congregations are wonderfully diverse. Mormons here are relatively few and far between, so congregations must draw on several communities for their memberships. Our ward draws its membership from no fewer than eleven towns! Several of those towns are wealthy suburban communities. A couple of them are middle class and comprised primarily of blue-collar workers. Our ward has many highly successful families (one might even call them Yuppies!). We have many people with advanced degrees. We have wonderful musicians and fine artists. We also have many laborers, both skilled and unskilled, and many whose education has been limited. We also have a wide range of ages and marital status. Our ward is not racially diverse but our stake is. We have the Boston Branch, which is largely African-American; a Cambodian branch, with members from throughout Southeast Asia; and a large Haitian population. We also have a thriving Spanish-speaking branch. Such diversity is not unusual in the Church, and I find it fascinating and rewarding to be part of it. The Church provides a great opportunity to expand our usually limited friendships to include people who are quite different from ourselves. Home teaching and visiting teaching assignments often pair us with people in different circumstances than our own. Use them. Befriend the families and individuals you teach. Invite them into your home. The older couple you visit might turn into foster grandparents for your children. Your home might be just the refuge needed by a college student away from home for the first time. The possibilities for members of diverse backgrounds to nurture one another are endless.

I cannot leave the subject of friendship without discussing one great hindering issue, that of time. The fast pace of contemporary life has taken a tremendous toll on people's abilities to make and sustain friendships. As a result, many people who are surrounded by large families are still impoverished for friends. Marriage and children cannot meet all our emotional needs. We need a variety of people in our lives, and even one close friend can be a great blessing. We do ourselves a great disservice if we become too neglectful of our friends. Moreover, we don't have to become neglectful of friends. Time can be taken even in the busiest of lives—time for a phone call, time for a neighborly chat across the fence, time for a postcard, and, occasionally, time for lunch or an evening together. We must do it for ourselves. We must do it for each other. If we neglect friendships, we run the risk of becoming ingrown and shriveled or lonely and embittered.

In this troubled world, we could all use someone with whom we can talk freely; we could all use more acceptance and openness; we could all use more understanding; we could all use more tolerance. We often find it is our friends who lift us out of our troubles, helping us reach heights we could never attain on our own.

PART 3:
MAGNIFYING SPIRITUAL GROWTH

Chapter 6: Repentance

In this life many things happen in which we play a shameful part. Those of us who are strong forgive ourselves and go on. The weak wallow in their shame and allow it to devour them. There is no one of us without sin, child. There ought to be some comfort in that. . . . Change is an easy thing to decide and a difficult thing to do. It is the day-to-day struggle of it that defeats people. Do not despair if old ways look good to you. Despair only if you fall into them too often.

KARLEEN KOEN

A FEW MONTHS AGO I attended a stake conference. The theme was repentance. Six men and women spoke during the session. Without exception, the speakers introduced their talks with the comment that they were addressing only those in the congregation who had committed serious transgressions and were thus in need of repentance. The implication was that the rest of us were fine and need not concern ourselves with repentance. We all know that is not true, and yet we often talk, think, and act as if it were.

What is repentance, and what does it have to do with the average, active, commandment-keeping Latter-day Saint? And more in keeping with the theme of this book, how does repentance relate to the experiences of our daily lives?

In the Church we speak of the process of repentance as involving four essential steps:

1. Recognize wrongdoing (sin).
2. Experience Godly sorrow for sin.
3. Ask for forgiveness and, where possible, make restitution.
4. Forsake the sin and never repeat it.

Recognizing Wrongdoing (Sin)

The speakers at stake conference made their mistakes at step one. So do most of us. When we think of sin, we usually think of the "biggies": adultery, dishonesty, breaking the Word of Wisdom, child abuse, inactivity, and so on. There are problems with that way of thinking about sin. The first problem is that many of us use these sins to excuse ourselves from thinking seriously about our own sins; these are sins somebody else commits. The second problem is that when we think of sin in that way, we narrow our perception of sins to actions only; we completely overlook the role of thoughts, attitudes, and motivations. Yet the scriptures make clear that, even in the midst of doing right, we can *be* wrong.

The Apostle Paul wrote of the last days, "Men shall be lovers of their own selves, covetous, boasters, proud, blasphemers, disobedient to parents, unthankful, unholy, without natural affection, trucebreakers, false accusers, incontinent, fierce, despisers of those that are good, traitors, heady, highminded, lovers of pleasures more than lovers of God." (2 Timothy 3:2–4.)

The sins of action listed here are bragging, blaspheming, disobedience, dishonesty, and slander. The sins of being are selfishness, envy, pride, ingratitude, conceit, and hedonism. Who among us can honestly say we are free from selfishness, envy, pride, or conceit? More disturbing still, our good actions are sometimes motivated by sins of being, by envy, conceit, competitiveness, or self-righteousness. But does motivation matter? And if so, how much?

In "Murder in the Cathedral," by T. S. Eliot, Thomas Becket has a fascinating struggle with a person (himself) described as "the tempter." Thomas Becket's struggle with himself centers around his motivations for making a choice that might result in his martyrdom:

> TEMPTER: What can compare with glory of Saints
> Dwelling forever in presence of God?
> What earthly glory, of king or emperor,

What earthly pride, that is not poverty
Compared with richness of heavenly grandeur?
Seek the way of martyrdom, make yourself the
     lowest
On earth, to be high in heaven.
And see far off below you, where the gulf is fixed,
Your persecutors, in timeless torment,
Parched passion, beyond expiation.

THOMAS: No!
Who are you, tempting with my own desires? . . .
Others offered real goods, worthless
But real. You only offer
Dreams to damnation.

TEMPTER: You have often dreamt them.

THOMAS: Is there no way, in my soul's sickness,
Does not lead to damnation in pride?
I well know that these temptations
Mean present vanity and future torment.
Can sinful pride be driven out
Only by more sinful? Can I neither act nor suffer
Without perdition? . . .
The last temptation is the greatest treason:
To do the right deed for the wrong reason. . . .
To become servant of God was never my wish.
Servant of God has chance of greater sin
And sorrow, than the man who serves a king.
For those who serve a greater cause
     may make the cause serve them.[1]

Becket was tempted to make a right choice, martyrdom, not
because it was the right thing to do, but because it would earn
him eternal glory and lead to the damnation of his enemies.
Before he could "choose the right" and have that choice *be* truly
right, he had to rid his heart of pride and the desire for revenge.
Motivation matters.

An interesting commentary on the significance of motivation in right- and wrongdoing is seen in the beliefs about heaven held by the followers of Emanuel Swedenborg. Swedenborg describes an afterlife remarkably similar to our own understanding, complete with three degrees of glory: a telestial kingdom, a terrestrial kingdom, and a celestial kingdom. Entrance to any of these kingdoms, he says, is not dependent upon good works or compliance with the performance of ordinances. It is assumed that all who enter any of the three kingdoms have participated in required ordinances and spent their lives engaged in good works, for these are three levels of heaven. The determining factor for an individual's final destination is not the quality or quantity of good works performed but rather the motivation behind them. Those going to the telestial kingdom are those whose good deeds are motivated by a sense of duty; those going to the terrestrial kingdom are those motivated by a love of truth; those invited into the celestial kingdom are those motivated by a love for God. Sense of duty, love of truth, and love for God—all three of these motivations are righteous. If I could get to the point in my own life where all my actions were motivated by one of these three, I would have come a long way in my own spiritual progression. The sins Paul lists in 2 Timothy, envy, pride, ingratitude, conceit, and love of pleasure, are just a few of the "sins of being/motivation" human beings are prone to. We could add selfishness, laziness, fearfulness, lust, and greed. It would require an entire book to discuss each of these. I have chosen three—pride, fear, and laziness—that I would like to discuss to help us begin to overcome these problems and to illustrate that repentance is a complex and life-long effort.

Pride, Fear, and Laziness: The Problems

President Benson identified pride as the universal sin. But what is pride? How does the pride that is harmful differ from healthy self-esteem? What of the feeling of calm confidence that accompanies right doing? Is that pride? What of the powerful ego that is often seen in effective leaders, even righteous leaders? Is that pride? I'm not sure I have answers to those questions. I am neither a psychologist nor a theologian. But I do have some ideas based on my own experiences with both the good and bad aspects of pride. It seems to me that self-esteem, calm confidence from right doing, and strong egos are all based on one thing—the truth. They are based on the truth because people with high self-esteem and strong egos are people who know and accept the truth about themselves. Their self-esteem is based on personal integrity. Moreover, self-esteem is often accompanied by sincere humility and a sense of deep gratitude to God.

The kind of pride President Benson referred to is often called false pride. It is based on pretense. In some ways we all fall short, we all disappoint ourselves. We use false pride to shelter ourselves from our disappointment. The more honest we are, the more self-esteem we have and the more capable we are of accepting our shortcomings with grace or even humor. But to some degree we all cover up. We use many techniques to cover our self-disappointment and soothe our wounded self-esteem. We put on fancy clothes and gather possessions. We criticize, judge, and gossip. We join cliques, eager to associate with the bright, the witty, and the beautiful, eager to avoid the slow or unattractive. False pride seeks to build up and exalt a false sense of self-goodness, often at the expense of others.

Self-esteem often seeks cooperation and the common good. False pride almost always contains an element of competition. Competition may be great when playing games, but it has no place in the personal relationships within a religious community such as our wards.

A wonderful sister in our ward has spent the past several years studying the New Testament. She has taken many courses at Wellesley College and Harvard in both the New Testament and Greek. She has often shared what she has learned with our ward or stake in Gospel Doctrine and Relief Society lessons, Women's Conference addresses, and special classes she has offered. When she was studying the letters of Paul, she often told us of Paul's insistence that we remove competition from our relationships. In fact, charity was defined as "seeking the good of the other without competition or proving." Think about that—to seek the good of another without competition or trying to prove anything. Think about your daily interactions with other people at work, school, home, or church. At work, could you seek the good of your customers or co-workers with no thought given to competing with co-workers or proving something to your boss? At school, could you learn for the sake of learning, help fellow students for the sake of helping, and remove competitiveness from your relationships? At home, could you seek the good of your spouse, children, parents, or siblings without competing with someone or trying to prove yourself? At church, could you help another for the sake of helping and remove "keeping up with the Joneses," "in-groups," and "out-groups" from your ward? Thinking about these situations makes me feel discouraged, as I do when someone quotes the scripture "Be ye therefore perfect." Removing pride, competitiveness, and proving from our motivations would require extraordinary effort! And so I lament, and maybe you do too, with Thomas Beckett, "Can sinful pride be driven out?"

Fear is the second problem on our list.

Fear is the opposite of faith. In *Lectures on Faith*, Joseph Smith says, "Faith is the principle of action in all intelligent beings. Faith . . . is the moving cause of all action."[2] Faith is a principle of action. Fear then, as the opposite of faith, is a principle of inaction. Fear is the motivation for our sins of omission. Unlike pride, fear itself is not a sin. In fact, the definition of courage is to act in the face of fear. The motivation and strength to act in the face of fear come from faith.

Fear is as common to the human condition as is pride. The story of Job points out some interesting things about fear. Job was a man of God, successful in the community, a strong family man, and a spiritually centered man. Yet when misfortune began to assail him, one of the first things he said was, "The thing which I greatly feared is come upon me." (Job 3:25.) In spite of his faith, a faith that eventually triumphed in his life, Job was beset by hidden and secret fears. So are we all.

Like Job, many of us fear loss: loss of material possessions; loss of a family member through death, disease, or sin; loss of status; loss of security.

Most of us also fear exposure. We want to appear competent and capable, yet we don't always feel that way. We often feel weak, vulnerable, and inadequate, and we fear that others will discover our weakness. So we hide. We become super-people, hiding behind a mask of extraordinary capability or worldly achievement, or we become shy and hide behind a thin veneer of meekness. We hide from others and we hide from ourselves; perhaps most significantly, we hide from God. We don't want anyone to discover our vulnerability. But then, horror of horrors, like Job's, our fears come upon us, and we are exposed for all the world to see. Our children grow up and become teenagers, they grow restless and unhappy, they become rebellious or get into trouble—and they don't even have the decency to do it in the privacy of our homes. They do it publicly, for all the world to see. Or, the children we desperately hoped for don't materialize. Or the economy goes through a recession and we lose our jobs, our homes, or our life's savings. Or we move into our thirties or forties and it becomes obvious to all that we're not going to marry. Or we get fat or go bald or lose our health, or all three! The list could go on and on, for the fact is, we are all human. We are all vulnerable, and, at some point in our lives, our fears do come upon us. We are exposed for what we are: sometimes good, sometimes not so good, sometimes strong, sometimes weak, sometimes capable, sometimes inadequate, sometimes courageous, often afraid.

Though fear most often leads to sins of omission, it can also lead to dishonesty or deceit. Afraid of punishment, criticism, ridicule, or exposure, we lie. We lie to others and we lie to ourselves. Fear is not so much a sin to be repented of as an obstacle to overcome on the path of repentance. The first step is the same as the first step in all repentance: to identify the problem. We must look within ourselves to discover (uncover) our fears. We then must face and accept them, look them right in the eye, and say, "Yes! You are mine. You are a part of who I am!" Only then can we begin to make overcoming our fears part of our process of repentance.

The final sin I would like to discuss, a sin as universal as both pride and fear, is laziness. I would like to quote from M. Scott Peck's *The Road Less Traveled*. Here he is discussing the causes of sin:

> Our failure to conduct—or to conduct fully and wholeheartedly—this internal debate between good and evil is the cause of those evil actions that constitute sin. In debating the wisdom of a proposed course of action, human beings routinely fail to obtain God's side of the issue. They fail to consult or listen to the God within them, the knowledge of rightness which inherently resides within the minds of all [human beings]. We make this failure because we are lazy. It is work to hold these internal debates. They require time and energy just to conduct them. And if we take them seriously—if we seriously listen to this "God within us"—we usually find ourselves being urged to take the more difficult path, the path of more effort rather than less. To conduct the debate is to open ourselves to suffering and struggle. Each and every one of us, more or less frequently, will hold back from this work, will also seek to avoid this painful step. Like Adam and Eve, and every one of our ancestors before us, we are all lazy.[3]

Here, then, is the essence of our problems with repentance. It is so much easier to think of repentance as something someone else needs. It is so much easier to define the big sins only. But if we have to examine our motives even for our good deeds, if we have to uncover and face our fears, if we have to conduct the "internal debate"—that's hard and often painful work! Yet it is work in which we must be constantly engaged. We must be engaged because *repentance* is simply another word for spiritual growth—growth toward God, and, unfortunately, if we are not growing toward God, we are growing away from him. In the final analysis it comes down to this—we succumb to our laziness or we begin the task of repentance, of examining our motives and confronting our fears.

Pride, Fear, Laziness: Some Help

Regular self-examination is the first step on the road of repentance. To conduct the "internal debate": What did I do today? How was I feeling while I was doing it? How did I feel afterward? Was I judgmental, self-congratulatory, or smug? What did I fail to do? What were my motives? Was I afraid? Was I lazy or were there other priorities? Am I being too hard on myself?—not in this context; this is the time to let yourself be filled with self-doubt.

Regularly spending time in this kind of self-examination accomplishes more than just recognition of sin. The very act of examining ourselves and our motives diminishes pride and increases humility. The act of discovering our fears itself requires courage. And the whole process is hard work that requires great self-discipline. Just by beginning, we find ourselves moved down the road toward our goal. As we become more conscious of our pride, our fears, and our laziness, we become uncomfortable. We respond to that discomfort in one of two ways: either we stop doing the self-examination and hide from ourselves, or we act. Action is the next step in the process of repentance.

Confess, Ask Forgiveness, Forsake Sin?

These final three steps of repentance are pretty straightforward when one thinks of sins as wrong*doing*, but when sin is defined in terms of motives and fears, things become a little more complex. How does one forsake pride, fear, or laziness? Let me illustrate just how difficult this is with the problem of pride.

Here we are on a bright, sunny Monday morning. We said our prayers this morning. We confessed our pride and our competitiveness to God and asked his forgiveness. We got up determined to free our behavior from all misguided or self-seeking motivations. We get to work (it could be school or parenting) and start by offering today's efforts to the glory of God. We're doing well. We've never been quite so productive or cheerful as we work. Then the boss comes by, pats us on the back, and compliments our efforts; or maybe the boss doesn't even notice our efforts; or maybe someone at the next desk is looking at us as if we're crazy; or maybe we notice we're doing twice as much as anyone else in the room. Now the trouble begins. Little thoughts just pop up into our minds. Thoughts like "Ha, I'll show Joe (or the boss) who does the best work around here" or "Why don't they quit talking and get to work. Do I have to do everything around here?" and then "Oh no! I wasn't going to be this way today."

Pride, fear, and laziness are not easy to forsake. All three seem to grow within our hearts, minds, and habits like weeds in a garden. How do we forsake and never repeat those kinds of sins? We don't forsake. We grow. And, like all growing things, we do it just a little at a time. With grosser sins repentance is forsaking; more often repentance is growing—slowly growing away from sin and toward God. However, there are actions we can take and techniques we can use to move the process along. We've already mentioned two. The first is regular self-examination, the second is prayer. There are other techniques for each problem, and I will discuss them one at a time.

Pride

I have a friend who is a physical therapist. She recently told me a wonderful story of an incident at her work. Her "sin" or "wrong way of being" was not so much competition or proving as it was self-involvement at an inappropriate time. Our egos have many ways of interfering, and pride wears many masks.

She was with an elderly patient in the patient's hospital room. She was putting her patient through a series of therapeutic exercises. However, she was not "with" the patient. As she worked, her mind was with the next patient, and the next, reviewing her afternoon, filled with herself. She suddenly became conscious of that and was slightly embarrassed, feeling she was slighting her patient in some way. She prayed, saying, "Dear Lord, how would *you* be if *you* were here treating this patient?" Immediately her mind shifted, but not in the way she expected. She thought she might imagine herself as the Savior treating the patient; instead, in her mind, her patient *became* the Savior. This patient had my friend's full attention now! During the rest of the therapy session my friend treated her patient with the same gentle, tender touch and full attention she would have given a newborn baby. When the session was over, the patient complimented my friend on her kindness. Neither the good deed nor the praise received prompted feelings of pride in my friend. She felt as if she had participated in a sacred experience and left the room feeling both humble and grateful.

A similar story is told of Mother Teresa of Calcutta. A patient was waiting to be treated. The patient had an ugly, filthy wound crawling with maggots. The young nun who was assigned to treat the patient could not bring herself to touch the wound; she shrank in revulsion. Mother Teresa gave the young nun a look of mild reproof and said gently, "My dear, this is Jesus." She then proceeded to cleanse and dress the wound herself.

Imagine doing all your work or good deeds as if to or for the Savior. Where is there room for feelings of competition or proving? When your work or service are done and they are good, they are just that. Good. And you don't feel pride, for you've only been a vehicle, a conduit for the Lord. You feel privileged, you feel humble, and you feel grateful.

A second technique is to avoid too much struggling with your pride. Bring it to awareness, become conscious of it, but don't fight it. Instead replace it. We need to realize when competition or proving enters the picture, but then we need to immediately shift our attention to the first part—seeking the good of the other. In the first illustration—the one at the office—what might our response to our co-workers be if we remembered to seek the good for them? In parenting or marriage, friendship or church service, what might we be like if we reminded ourselves to seek the good of the other? In the context of work or home, seeking the good of another might sometimes require confrontation or honest expression of anger. The key is to first examine our motives and then speak with the benefit of the other foremost in our minds.

Fear

We've already discussed one of the major antidotes for fear. We've all heard the truism "to banish fear you must do the thing you fear." This is extremely difficult, for we all shrink from doing that which we fear. It is best to start small, using self-examination to set short-term goals for actions that help counter fears. Start with sins of omission. You might visit or home teach a less-active but not hostile member to help overcome anxiety about sharing the gospel; bear your testimony more often; if you are shy, introduce yourself to one person you don't know each month; if you are outgoing, move beyond your close circle of friends to regularly invite the elderly, single, or less active into your home. These types of things, and many more, can be used to extend ourselves, to regularly act in the face of small fears and anxieties so that faith and action gradually replace and minimize fears. As our fears are reduced, we become more spontaneous, and we are freer to act in response to promptings of the Spirit. The importance of challenging ourselves in this way cannot be overemphasized. Thinking about spiritual growth, thinking about repentance, is an important first step, but it has no value unless it is followed by action. Consider this advice exchanged between two devils concerning a man who had a recent profound spiritual experience:

> The great thing is to prevent his doing anything.
> As long as he does not convert it into action, it does
> not matter how much he thinks about this new repen-
> tance. Let the little brute wallow in it. Let him, if he
> has any bent that way, write a book about it; that is
> often an excellent way of sterilising the seeds which
> the Enemy plants in a human soul. Let him do any-

> thing but act. No amount of piety in his imagination
> and affections will harm us if we can keep it out of his
> will. . . . The more often he feels without acting, the
> less he will be able ever to act, and, in the long run,
> the less he will be able to feel.[4]

When you feel afraid—act. When you feel compassion—act. When you feel offended, hurt, or angry—speak up. When you see a problem that needs correcting—act. When your children need a lesson on a particular subject—prepare the lesson and present it at family night. The more often you act on hunches, insights, or promptings, ignoring any fear or reticence that may come up, the less often you will be afraid. A word of warning—don't get so carried away you become insensitive; sometimes *not* acting is an act of kindness.

Action is the solution when we are afraid of doing. We have discussed other kinds of fear as well, primarily fear of exposure. We are afraid of exposing ourselves as vulnerable and imperfect. This type of fear can be a real problem in the Church. We are a people who value success. We have the "Molly Mormons" and the "Perfect Pauls," super-moms and super-dads who are super successful.

We often see each other only at church events in our "Sunday best." We often assume that "Sunday best" is an honest reflection of everyone else, while we know it is not an honest reflection of ourselves.

"If they only knew what my life was really like," we think.

Well—what if they knew?

What then?

Would we be excommunicated? "Banned from Boston?" I doubt it. If they only knew—if we only let them know. If we all let each other know our truer selves, we might have more of a wonderful thing called community. Letting others know our real selves used to be called confession. It used to be public, and when it went private a few hundred years after Christ's death, a great tool for repentance and personal growth was lost. I have a born-again Christian friend named Lisa. Lisa has testimony meeting at the church she attends, as do we. Her testimony meetings are a little different from ours. They don't bear testimony of their church or their leaders. They don't bear testimony that God lives or that Jesus is the Christ; these are assumed common knowledge. Instead they bear testimony of God working in their lives, of his power, and they start with a confession. When Lisa bears her testimony, she tells her entire conversion story. It is quite a story, complete with alcohol, drugs, and homosexuality, all repented of with God's help. The first time she bore her testimony, she was understandably nervous. We talked about it the following week. She told me of others who had born their testimonies the same day. I particularly remember the story of one man. He could be any one of us. He was a successful businessman and was highly esteemed in the congregation. He had suffered severe financial losses. He began his testimony by telling of those losses. He did not go on to tell how God had saved him from financial disaster. Instead, he talked of how God had used his financial crisis to reveal to him his own weaknesses. Because of his financial setback, he had become aware of his attachment to material things and of an insidious form of pride and arrogance that often accompanies financial success. He openly confessed these traits and apologized to any in the congregation he might have hurt. Then he thanked his Heavenly Father for the valuable lesson. My friend Lisa and this man had nothing to fear because they had nothing to hide. For Jesus' sake, they were willing to open their lives to be examined by the members of their congregation. In so doing, they exercised their faith, casting themselves upon God's mercy and the mercy of their fellow parishioners. They also opened the way for fellow parishioners to offer support, encouragement, forgiveness, and love.

Contrast this with a recent experience of a member of my ward. This woman was relatively new in our ward. We were having a joint Relief Society–priesthood meeting, and the subject for discussion was depression. During the lesson, this new member of our ward raised her hand and shared her personal struggles with depression. In private after the lesson, another member of our congregation reproached this woman, telling her that she had made a "serious mistake" in being so open.

Experiences like this cause *me* to fear. I fear it will be a long time before Mormon congregations and communities open up. How do we overcome fear living in a culture that wears an "all is well" mask? We have to start small, and we can. We can be more open at home, thus making our relationships there more honest and more intimate. We can be more open with our close friends, expressing fears and confiding failures and weaknesses. We might have difficulty being open in testimony meeting but find it easier in priesthood or Relief Society lessons. It might help us if we remember that wearing that "all is well" mask is known as hypocrisy in the scriptures.

Fear is the opposite of faith. Action and confession are acts of faith. We must begin somewhere, for just as we cannot love God if we don't love our fellowman, we cannot pretend to have faith in God if we don't have faith in each other.

Laziness

The final sin we must grow out of if we are to grow toward God is laziness. The answer to laziness is self-discipline. Self-discipline is the bedrock on which all other repentance rests. All of the steps we've been describing here—self-examination, monitoring our thoughts and motivations, replacing pride with humility and gratitude, reducing competitiveness, acting in the face of fear, and confessing our vulnerability to each other—all require self-discipline. All these steps require hard work and great effort. All these steps are painful, and our natural tendency is to avoid them. We build and strengthen our self-discipline, and thus repent of laziness, every time we repent of pride or fear. Self-discipline is an aspect of repentance that we must exercise if we are to have any hope of truly repenting, of growing toward God. What will help us with this arduous task? Where do we get the motivation to embark and strength to continue on the road of repentance? The motivation is provided by love, love for

ourselves, love for the precious people in our lives, and, ulti-
mately, love for God.

"The stranger and the enemy, we saw him in the mirror." To
look in that mirror and begin to deal with what we see there can
be terrifying, but we are sustained even as we tremble. We are sustained by our love for God and our intense desire to be with him
again; we are sustained by a sure knowledge of his love for us; we
are sustained by grace. Being sustained, we look, and looking, we
begin. The process of repentance has begun—rest assured, in this
lifetime, it will never end.

Chapter 7: Service

Caring is the greatest thing, caring matters most.

—FREDERICK VON HUGEL (LAST WORDS)

SOME YEARS AGO I experienced a "spiritual crisis." I wasn't sure anymore. I found myself at the periphery of ward activity. My questions and troubled countenance set me apart, and people began to avoid me. I was often without a car, and it became difficult to get rides to Relief Society. I called the friends who had always been willing to help before, but cars were suddenly full. I was determined to attend and went so far as putting my baby in my bicycle basket and riding my bike to Relief Society. I felt hurt, though, and began to tire of the effort. One Tuesday I decided just to skip it. A little after noon, my doorbell rang. On my front step stood Caroline, a sister from my ward. She had just moved into the ward, and we didn't know each other very well. She had six children and was also without a car during the day. She had asked another sister to bring her to my home that day, drop her off, and pick her up again after our visit. She busied three young children with toys in my front yard and came in to talk. She had noticed that I was troubled, and she was concerned that I had not attended Relief Society that day. We talked at length. As she rose to go, she looked into my eyes and said, "Joan, I want you to know that for as long as you need me, I am going to be your guardian angel. You will be in my prayers morning and night. I will not let you falter." We cried, we embraced, and she left. The following Sunday, Caroline handed me an envelope, saying she had found a poem while cleaning and thought it might help me. I opened the envelope. It contained a scrap of paper, yellow and frayed with age. Written on it, in beautiful calligraphy, was this poem:

> Be like the bird which,
> pausing in its flight, on a limb too slight,
> feels it give way beneath him
> yet sings,
> Knowing he has wings.
>
> —VICTOR HUGO

I kept that poem in my purse for years and read it whenever I felt troubled. I survived my crisis, though I've not forgotten it. Neither have I forgotten the sweet sister who responded to the prompting of the Spirit and came to minister to me.

Many years later I had an opportunity to offer similar support to a co-worker. I didn't take it. I didn't take it because it came at a busy place during a busy time, and it was just so inconvenient! I didn't even see the problem as an opportunity for service. All I saw was the aggravation, until another co-worker addressed the problem, rendered the service, and left me feeling ashamed of myself.

I worked part-time from 3:00 to 11:00 P.M. in a hospital hematology lab. The troubled co-worker was new to our department. I'll call her Michelle. She trained for a few weeks on the day shift and was then moved onto the evening shift with me and another technician to complete her training. We knew she had problems when she began, but we didn't know how much they would interfere with her work. Her husband had left her three months earlier, on Christmas Eve! She had a seventeen-year-old daughter and a fourteen-year-old son. She was having serious difficulty with her son. He was angry, rebellious, and often deeply depressed. He would call her every night she worked, and they would argue over the phone for forty-five minutes to an hour. The phone calls destroyed Michelle. She would rave about her husband, complain about her son, wring her hands about her need to work the evening shift while leaving her son alone—and she would cry.

Invariably we sent her home between 8:00 and 9:00 in tears.
Then it was our turn to complain. Why did she have to bring her
problems to work with her? Why couldn't she accept reality and
work during the day shift when her son was in school so she could
be home in the evening when he needed her? And most of all,
how could she put *us* in such an awkward position! Eventually
Michelle had a nervous breakdown. I was not working the night
it happened, but I was there, visiting the lab with my daughter to
work on a science fair project. I saw Michelle's dazed expression,
I heard her crying, and I joined with fellow employees complain-
ing about her in the next room. A student, working her way
through college as a phlebotomist, came to Michelle's aid. The
student called around to find a replacement for Michelle, took
her to the emergency room, stayed with her until a psychiatrist
arrived, and made sure she had transportation home.

That was the beginning of Michelle's turnaround; she's been
through a lot, but she's fine now. I often wonder what might have
happened if Debbie, our student phlebotomist, had not been
there for her. Interestingly enough, Debbie was ostracized by her
co-workers that evening. She was told she shouldn't have gotten
involved—it was none of her business. I worked with Debbie
three days later. I complimented her on her actions. The rest of
us had offered judgment—she had offered help. She looked at me
and said, "You know I'm Catholic, and I take my religion seriously. I walked into this room and saw her sitting there looking
so miserable—my heart just went out to her. What else could I
do?" My *heart just went out to her.* "Good grief," I thought, "where
was my heart?"

Service. What kind of service does our Heavenly Father want
from us, and what does Heavenly Father want us to learn or gain
from the service we render to others? I believe that Heavenly
Father wants far more than our willing acceptance of Church
callings. I believe that what he wants most is illustrated in both of
these stories.

He wants our hearts.

He wants our hearts softened.

He wants our hearts open.

He wants our hearts, minds, schedules, and bodies, available and responsive.

A softened, open heart renders a type of service that has a unique characteristic—spontaneity. A softened, open heart is responsive to promptings of the Spirit and responsive to need. Service rendered is then both appropriate and timely. To give service spontaneously, responding to need at the time the need is expressed, is a tremendous challenge. The expressed need almost always takes us by surprise. It interferes with our busy schedules and intrudes upon our preoccupied minds. To render service responsively is *always* inconvenient. My friend not only inconvenienced herself to come to my aid, she also inconvenienced her children and the sister who was planning on driving her home. It was my very unwillingness to accept inconvenience that caused me to harden my heart to my co-worker's pain.

To render service responsively also entails risk and requires courage. Debbie was ostracized by co-workers for leaving her post to help another. When Caroline rang my doorbell, she had no idea how she would be received; she wasn't even sure I had a problem. All she knew was that I hadn't shown up on that particular Tuesday. I might have had a sick child, making her "rush to my rescue" seem melodramatic or ill-conceived. I might have greeted her with hostility or rejection. Stepping into the unknown to offer assistance to another is scary business, but step we must. The Savior admonishes us time and time again to serve one another. Some of that service is offered as we fill our callings and assignments in the Church, but more is needed. Responsiveness is needed. Open, tender hearts are needed. Caring is needed, for truly, in service, "Caring is the greatest thing, caring matters most."

Accepting Service from Others

Service is a two-way street. Sometimes we are the givers, but we all have problems and we all have pain. When it's our turn to suffer, we need to allow others the opportunity to serve. To decline offers of service from others is sin. The sin is pride, and it is contagious. If we put on the "I can handle it myself" front for others, others will put on the same front for us. Before long an entire congregation can be pretending and filled with isolated, fragmented individuals and families.

My visiting teacher has traveled a lot. Before moving into our ward, she spent several years in Germany. She often comments on the high level of spirituality she found there. She attributes that spirituality to the tradition of service within the ward. It was a military ward with members frequently moving in and out. When a family moved into the ward, members would gather to help wallpaper, paint, or drape the new member's home. When a family moved out, the members would gather to help pack and clean. My friend wasn't accustomed to this kind of help and politely declined the offers extended to her. She became quite ill, and the offers increased. She continued to decline. One Sunday she was called into the stake president's office (he was a personal friend and knew the situation). Gently at first and then with increasing sternness, he called my friend to repentance. He called her attention to the high level of spirituality in the ward. He pointed out the possibility that the spirituality was related to the tradition of service. He suggested that her unwillingness to accept service might be interfering with the Lord's work!

She changed and began to accept when members called with offers to help. Being ill, she was grateful for the help. Being humble, she was grateful for the lesson. She's never forgotten. She talked me into having a painting party when I was painting my living room, and she continues to believe that giving and accepting service are key elements of a healthy, spirit-filled congregation.

Community, Nation, and World

Latter-day Saints are busy folk. We're busy with our large families, we're busy with our Church callings, we're busy with our

LDS friends. Latter-day Saints are also responsible, sensitive, spiritual folk. Add up the two, and you get guilt. I've never known an active Mormon who didn't want to do more! In a way, our guilt is deserved. We have a reputation for taking good care of each other, but we often fall short in the area of community service. We have much more to offer than we often do. As I discuss service to the larger community, I hope to do two things: motivate at least some readers to serve in their communities, and provide reasonable guidelines for deciding where, when, and how much service to offer.

The Problem

Many who would serve don't, simply because the need is so great that they know neither where to begin nor where to stop. The problems in our communities, states, nations, and world are so large that even to begin to make a contribution seems like a full-time job. Or we feel defeated at the onset—the "what difference can one person make?" syndrome. Knowing I can't solve the whole problem, I do nothing. I heard a story at stake conference last year that speaks to this problem.

The story took place on a beach several miles long on the coast of Maine. A man was strolling along the beach the day after a storm. The storm had washed up a bed of starfish, and the beach was covered with hundreds of thousands of starfish, dying in the sun. As the man walked along, shaking his head in dismay, he came upon a small boy who was picking starfish up, one by one, and heaving them back into the ocean. The man stopped to talk.

"Too bad, eh?" he said.

"Yeah, they're going to die," the boy said as he tossed one back into the water.

"There must be thousands," said the man.

The boy surveyed the scene. "Maybe a million," he said as he tossed another one.

They stood silently for a few minutes as the boy threw three or four more back into the sea.

"Why do you bother?" asked the man. "You're not going to make any difference."

The boy looked down at the starfish in his hand. As he threw it into the ocean, he said, "I can make a difference to this one."

We can all make a difference for one.

I recently saw a book with an intriguing title: *All I Can Do Is All I Can Do and All I Can Do Is Enough*. We can evaluate commitments at home and church; we can determine all we can do and do it. Even if it is only three PTA meetings a year, if that is honestly all we can do, it is enough. At least for now.

What One Person Can Do

There are many factors to be considered before offering service in the community. I would like to consider four: personal interests, available time, personal talents and abilities, and, finally, opportunity.

Your personal interests should play an important role in choosing how you might serve in the community. I am not thinking of personal interests in terms of hobbies or activities you might enjoy. I am thinking more of social issues that you find yourself caring deeply about.

I have a burning issue. It is a problem in our communities and nation that "grabs" me. I become passionate whenever I talk to friends or neighbors about it. My burning issue is public education. There are other issues in our world that are more pressing, more urgent. There are many issues equally important. But they don't touch me the way "my" issue does. When feeling overwhelmed by the needs of our complicated world; when I see television programs or read newspaper articles about AIDS, the environment, pornography, drug abuse, homelessness, and so on, I remember two things: (1) all I can do is all I can do; and (2) right now only one issue really lights my fire, and that's where I choose to serve. When choosing where and how to offer your time, choose something personally meaningful to you. Work to solve problems you get worked up about. When we can bring passion and commitment to our service, the service will be far more effective and far more satisfying.

The second factor to consider when offering community service is available time.

"To every thing there is a season, and a time to every purpose under the heaven" is something I seemed to hear quoted in Relief Society at least once a month when my children were small. It didn't make me feel less guilty, only more impatient. Now that my children are all in school and I have a bit more time, I realize that it's true. Now I also realize that when you are conscientiously raising your children, you are already rendering a tremendous service to your community and nation.

I truly believe that parents are the only people who simply cannot afford much time to give to community service. Children at home connect us to a multitude of service opportunities—PTA, school volunteer programs, Boy and Girl Scouts, and so on—that we don't seem connected to when our children are grown and have left home. So parents have plenty of opportunity but not much time. Parents need to be careful to balance available time between parenting, Church callings, and community service. Attending a PTA meeting or spending an hour a week volunteering in the school library are activities almost any parent can do. Coaching a soccer team or becoming the PTA president, on the other hand, require much more time and energy and, therefore, more careful consideration before volunteering. Parents need to remember that their primary community service is in their own homes, and sometimes that has to be enough.

The single adult, the newly married childless couple, and the couple whose children have grown and left home often do have time. Some singles and elderly may even regard time not as a liability but as an asset. Many singles and retired people are lonely or find themselves with too much time on their hands. Singles who long for children, or the elderly who miss their children, can find great enrichment and personal satisfaction in the local school library or pediatrics ward. Foster parenting, grandparenting, and Big Brothers and Sisters offer similar opportunities for service to young people. Others might want to offer their time to their peers. Whatever your choice, the need is great, the opportunities endless, and the rewards rich and deep.

One last word about time. Sometimes the time is ripe when time doesn't seem available. Issues come and issues go, needs come and needs go. Problems arise and are sometimes solved. If you want to be part of the solution to a particular problem, you may have to act when the time is ripe, whether time is available or not. It can be done. Priorities can be rearranged and schedules reworked. Sometimes you just have to do what you have to do.

The third factor to consider when choosing community service is personal resources. By that I mean your personal talents, abilities, and relative wealth.

Where much is given, much is expected. Where a medium amount is given, a medium amount is expected. We can all serve in Primary, though we all don't have the ability to be Primary president. We can all talk to a troubled friend, though we all don't have the ability to be a bishop. Some can build a shelter for the homeless; others can only take their used clothing to the local Deseret Industries or Salvation Army. Don't feel guilty because you can't give what you don't possess! Don't judge others because they can give only what they do possess! Whether it is time, talent, leadership ability, or money, gear your contribution to your available resources and don't bite off more than you can chew. If, on the other hand, you can chew a lot, then—for heaven's sake—take a big bite!

The final factor to consider is opportunity. There is only one thing I want to say about opportunity: bloom where you are planted. It's hard to help with problems associated with declining inner city neighborhoods in Los Angeles, New York, or Boston if you live in a suburb of Provo. However, you can keep your own neighborhood clean and safe, and you can make sure there are plenty of wholesome activities for the young people growing up in your own neighborhood. The Savior set an example of the power inherent in serving in our own communities. He knew he was to be the Savior of the whole world, yet he did not leave

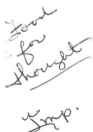
food for thought
Imp.

Israel and go off to Rome to find his mission. He stayed in the area of his own home and the context of his own culture. He confronted the evil he found there, he alleviated the suffering he met with, and he addressed the problems in his own community, in his own culture, and in his own religious institution. In so doing, he changed forever the social structure and ethical standards of an entire civilization. There is great power in small things. Heavenly Father doesn't ask us to change the world; he asks us to change our hearts. He asks us to care about and care for one another. He asks us to help. What else can we do?

Chapter 8: Grace

I was found of them that sought me not; I was made manifest unto them that asked not after me.

—ROMANS 10:20

IN DECEMBER 1989, we had a lovely Relief Society lesson on the Atonement. I gave the answer "grace" to a question asked by the teacher. I don't recall the question; if I did I would tell you what it was. I do recall the teacher's response to my answer. "Grace," she said. "That's a concept we don't talk about much in the Church. What does the word *grace* mean to you?" I sat speechless, trying to collect my thoughts about a word that melts my heart and brings sweetness to my soul every time I hear it. I could not answer her question then. I will attempt to answer it now.

The quotation from Romans that introduces this chapter expresses a universal truth, though somewhat obliquely: "I was found by those who sought me not." How can God be found by those who do not seek him? And for those who do seek God, where does the desire to seek him come from? And what about those who find God even as they run and hide from him? Whether we be seekers, indifferent, or runners, God always seeks us first. First, last, and always, in every circumstance and stage of our lives, our Heavenly Father strives to bring us to himself. Missionaries testify of this as they meet investigators who have often been seeking "something" for a long time, driven by a need that comes from beyond themselves. Members of the Church repenting of sins large or small will testify to this truth. Inactive members returning to activity will testify to this truth. Heavenly Father seeks after us always, nurturing us, prodding us, prompting us, correcting and inviting us. Moreover, unlike the gift of the Holy Ghost, this seeking does not seem to depend on any personal righteousness on our part. Indeed, it often comes when we are at our worst, farthest from God, or in dire straits, and it comes repeatedly, even if we continue in sin. Although, as the scriptures say, "the Spirit of God will not always strive with man," it has been my experience that the Spirit is not easily discouraged!

Grace Defined

Interestingly, this concept, this spiritual fact of life—that God meets us right where we are to bring us where he wants us to be—makes many Latter-day Saints uncomfortable. Where does that leave blessings predicated on obedience? What about keeping the commandments and those all-important works? Well, many blessings are predicated on obedience, and keeping the commandments and doing good works, are, of course, essential to living a spiritual life. But now we are talking about something else. We are talking about grace. Just what is grace anyway? Why is this concept so difficult to get a handle on? Why do Latter-day Saints tend to be so defensive about grace, immediately turning any meaningful discussion of grace into a discussion of works?

I'd like to start by mentioning what grace is not.

Grace is not faith. Grace, in fact, often precedes faith, even ignites faith. It often builds faith, but it is not faith.

Grace is not a free ride. Grace is the very experience that calls people to good works, and the experience of grace in the midst of sin can be an uncomfortable experience indeed. Grace is definitely not a free ride.

Grace is not salvation. Grace helps bring about salvation. Grace often opens people to the possibility of salvation, and, as we work out our salvation, grace supports and sustains us, prompts us, guides us, opens and closes doors, and picks us up when we get knocked down.

Grace is not exaltation, though without grace, exaltation is an impossibility.

Grace is not the Holy Ghost, gifts of the Spirit, or the light of Christ. The Holy Ghost, gifts of the Spirit, the light of Christ, faith, salvation, exaltation, and a host of other things are all manifestations of grace, but they are not, in themselves, grace.

What then, is grace?

In *Mormon Doctrine*, Elder Bruce R. McConkie defines grace in this way: "*God's grace* consists in his love, mercy, and condescension toward his children."[1]

In *The Road Less Traveled*, M. Scott Peck gives this definition: "Grace is a powerful force originating outside of human consciousness that nurtures the spiritual growth of human beings."[2]

"God's love, mercy, and condescension toward man." I've experienced that love, mercy, and condescension. So have you.

"A powerful force that nurtures the spiritual growth of human beings." I've experienced that powerful force—a force that has sometimes pulled, sometimes pushed, sometimes touched, sometimes opened doors, sometimes closed doors, sometimes opened or expanded my heart, my mind, or events in my life. Indeed, this force, this love, sometimes seems part of the very heartbeat of life.

As the Apostle Paul taught: "[God] made from one every nation of men to live on all the face of the earth, having determined allotted periods and the boundaries of their habitation, that they should seek God, in the hope that they might feel after him and find him. Yet he is not far from each one of us, *for 'in him we live and move and have our being.'*" (Acts 17:26–28, RSV; emphasis added.)

I believe that grace is the part of God in which we all live, move, and have our being. Like the water in which fishes swim, like the air we breathe, the grace of God is the medium in which human beings be.

Manifestations of Grace

If grace is the medium in which human beings be, then its manifestations must be many. They are many indeed. If we but open our eyes, we will find our world teeming with glorious manifestations of the grace of God.

All of creation testifies to the grace of God. The greenest greens, the bluest blues, the sparkle in the air on a sunny day, the incredible night sky, the rhythm of the seasons, all animal and plant life with its multiplicity and diversity, our own bodies and their intricate workings, the order found in nuclear physics—all manifest the glorious grace of God.

The plan of salvation and the atonement of Christ are manifestations of God's endless grace. We were loved, carefully nurtured, and prepared even in the premortal existence. When the plan of salvation was formed, all provision was made for us to be able to return to our Heavenly Father. Christ carefully prepared himself so he could come to earth and successfully complete his pain-filled mission—a mission that ended with his freely offering his life, while his Father looked on, held back, and suffered with him, that we might someday return to him.

The image of our heavenly parents painfully watching as careless and evil people crucified the Savior brings to mind another manifestation of grace, a manifestation that has brought chaos, evil, and much suffering into the world and yet stands as one of God's greatest gifts—the gift of agency. The right to choose and be self-determinant, to seek knowledge and understanding in our own way and at our own pace, to even turn away from goodness and from God himself, is a gift beyond description. Granting human beings agency requires Heavenly Father's continual self-discipline and guarantees his ongoing suffering and pain, for even though he could, and even though to do so would ease suffering, many times God simply will not intervene in the affairs of men.

Although to preserve our agency, God will not often intervene in our affairs uninvited, his involvement in the lives of those who seek him is remarkable. In the opening paragraphs of this chapter, I described God's willingness to work with us when we seek after him. The beatitudes state, "Blessed are they which do hunger and thirst after righteousness: for they shall be filled." (Matthew 5:6.) Grace says that the hungering and thirsting are themselves gifts from God. And after the hungering and thirsting, we are filled—we become more righteous. How do we become more righteous? First, we desire to—we hunger and thirst for grace. And then we work to become more righteous, and that too is prompted by and filled with grace.

Indeed, Heavenly Father's grace permeates and surrounds us, informing everything we do—all thought, all feeling, all experience, and all our work. If we, as Latter-day Saints, attempt to separate grace and works, we are doomed to fail and to expose ourselves as naive or arrogant or both.

As the Psalmist sang:

> Whither shall I go from thy spirit?
> Or whither shall I flee from thy presence?
> If I ascend up into heaven, thou art there:
> If I make my bed in hell, behold, thou art there;
> If I take the wings of the morning,
> And dwell in the uttermost parts of the sea,
> Even there shall thy hand lead me,
> And thy right hand shall hold me.
>
> (PSALM 139:7–10.)

Grace always precedes good works; always supports, sustains, and smooths out good works; and always follows good works, just as good works are our main response to grace. I've seen this acted out with the bold strokes of a wonderful work of art in the life of a friend.

Grace and Works

First, I'd like to qualify my definition of good works. When we think about good works, we usually think of service, and rightly so. But here, I'd like to talk about another kind of work, a work that is far more challenging for most of us than service. That work is the work of our own salvation.

The relationship between grace and the work of our own salvation is like building a stairway. Grace is the ground on which we stand, supporting us and prompting our upward gaze. With the desire and insight grace affords us, we build a step (work); with the strength grace supplies us, we step up (work); with more grace and more work we build another, step up and build another, and so on throughout our lives.

In the case of my friend Lisa, she started out on shaky ground indeed. She had been raised in an alcoholic home and grew up to be an angry young woman. She smoked, drank heavily, used marijuana and cocaine, and was sexually promiscuous. She didn't "fit in," and she wasn't interested in "getting along." A couple of years after I met Lisa, she met a young man who was a born-again Christian studying for the ministry. This young man worked part-time at our place of business for about six months. After work, on his last day, he invited Lisa outside. They went to his car, and he spent three hours reading over the scriptures with her. When they were done, Lisa bowed her head and said a prayer, accepting Christ as her Savior. She was born again—moved from sin to grace—and then the work began: arduous, painful, sometimes excruciating work, with frequent stops to fill up with much-needed grace.

She started by trying to read the Bible regularly. She would do okay for a while and then fall back, or misplace her Bible, or leave for a weekend vacation intending to spend the entire time reading but leaving her scriptures at home. Still, she kept trying and prayed for help. Within six months, she was reading scriptures regularly. She had built step one.

Next, she took on her bad habits—and failed miserably. Determined, she visited a counselor at work. He told her she couldn't begin to change until she stopped her substance abuse. He challenged her to not use marijuana for one week. She succeeded. He continued to counsel with her and help her until she had succeeded in giving up all drugs except for cigarettes.

She began to search for a church and set a baptismal date for about a year from her first prayer in our friend's car. She set a date to quit smoking, and this time she succeeded. Now she faced a different problem. Her changes began to catch up with her, and she became depressed. In spite of her newfound faith, her life became flat and empty. She continued to pray and study the scriptures. She expressed her faith frequently. She was saved by grace, she had made many changes in her life through grace, and she was confident that grace would get her through her depression. She never spoke of how hard she had worked; she only occasionally complained of the pain she was enduring; she frequently attributed her success to God's grace.

Time went on, and she continued her work. She found a new therapist and joined a support group. She was baptized. She and a friend started a Bible study class at a local youth detention center. Gradually her depression lifted, and we began to see a whole new personality emerge, not quite as lively as before, but warmer, more caring, and more concerned with others. It was about three years after her conversion experience. I would often look at her and marvel at the growth and change she had achieved in such a short time. When I voiced my feelings, she quickly assured me that she had done nothing on her own; it was all through the grace of God. Still, I had seen how hard she had worked—or at least I thought I had. Little did I know.

One night, Lisa and I were working alone together. We were discussing TV talk shows and their frequent homosexual themes. We then began discussing homosexuality in general. I told her about Carol Lynn Pearson's book *Goodbye, I Love You* and how her husband felt so strongly that homosexuality was a part of his nature that he needed to explore it and figure it out. She said,

"God doesn't make homosexuals. Homosexuality is a dysfunc-
tion." She then gave a plausible explanation of how and why it
develops. She paused and said, "I should know. I'm gay." My jaw
dropped. My heart stopped. I couldn't say anything—so she did.
She told me the rest of her story.

She told me of her struggles in the early days following her
conversion. She told me of her pain when she severed all her former relationships and moved out of her apartment to start a new
life. She told me of the support group for homosexual Christians
that had helped her gain both spiritual and psychological understanding. She told me of her fear and anxiety when, just prior to
her baptism, she shared the fact of her homosexuality with a
friend from the congregation she was joining, and of her relief
and joy when her friend assured her of Christ's love and acceptance of her with whatever problems or flaws she had. She told of
her despair and discouragement when, several months after her
baptism, she slipped into an affair with another young woman
from the congregation. She told of her repentance and continued
counseling with both professional counselors and her pastor. And
she taught me about grace—the grace that had brought her to
Christ three years before; the grace that had showed her which
step needed to be taken next; the grace that had opened doors
and put just the right people in her life just when she was ready
for what those people had to offer; the grace that had strengthened, supported, and comforted her as she had worked through
the long process of her repentance and change.

I felt the Spirit as she shared her story with me, and when she
was done, we worked in silence. After a while, she said, "Joan,
you're awfully quiet. What are you thinking?" I had to tell her. I
looked right into her eyes and said, "I feel like I'm in the presence
of a holy work. When God makes his presence known, when we
feel his Spirit right here with us—well, silence seems appropriate." We just looked at each other for a minute, and then we
smiled.

Today Lisa has gone back to school. She is majoring in psychology and hopes to become a Christian counselor. She is

engaged to be married to a fine young man from her congregation. Her fiancé knows her history and shares her commitment to continued growth. They continue to receive counseling both from their pastor and professionals. Lisa's life as a Christian will probably never be easy. Her disturbed past will probably continue to cast shadows on her life. There will always be struggle. Yet, she has great faith, and so do I, that through the grace of God, and her own willingness to work, she will make it.

Grace and Daily Living

In the beginning of this chapter, I compared grace to air and water. Here, I admit there are some problems with that analogy. Air and water are not only equally available to the life forms living in them, but they also permeate that life. To turn from them, to shut them out, is to die. We have no real choice but to use and be affected by them. Not so grace. Although I believe grace is equally available to all human beings, and that it can surround and permeate us, it can also be refused. We can, and many do, live oblivious to grace. We can, and many do, turn away from grace. We can, and many do, grow in grace.

The question then becomes, for seekers of greater spiritual growth, what specific things can we do to help us increase in grace? Can we bring more grace to our works and more work to our grace? I believe we can, and I believe that is best done in the context of our daily lives.

Think about the times in your life when you have felt the Spirit. Think about the times in sacrament or testimony meeting, baptismal services, or the temple. Then think about how you were living three days later. Were those Spirit-filled moments life-changing? Probably not. They are often comforting, often inspiring, but usually quite transient, temporary, isolated experiences with little impact on the reality of our daily lives. We need to bring that spirit into our daily lives. We need to become conscious of and responsive to the grace that is ever present. If we can't, of what use is our religion?

Sara Wenger Shenk wrote:

> Where can ordinary folk find a theology which springs from our everyday tasks and returns to invigorate us right where we are? My sense is that either faith must give me food for the road on a blurred, beleaguered morning, or it might as well . . . be stashed between two gilded book covers and set on a museum shelf to molder.
>
> If it isn't possible to know the quickening presence of God in the everyday routine, one might as well ship religiosity off to a seminary library and leave it there. Either God is the God of all life, or God is on the reserve shelf, available and relevant only to a sanctified elite.[3]

When Jesus taught his followers, did he expound and theologize? Did he take them into the synagogue and temple and teach great and complex doctrines? Did he even commonly lead them in prayer? No, he did not. Jesus taught his followers using stories, stories based on the common, the down-to-earth, and the everyday. He used images of the housewife sweeping, the shepherd, the fisherman, and the farmer. He lit lamps, removed splinters from eyes, built houses, and planted seeds. He used the knowable experiences of our daily lives to grant us glimpses of the grace of God.

The fact is, increasing in grace is not only best done in the context of our daily lives; it actually cannot be done anywhere else. And there are concrete steps we can take to help.

Many of these steps have already been discussed, but I'd like to restate them here in the context of growing in grace.

We can, and many do, live our lives oblivious to grace. The first step in changing that is to become more conscious of grace, to increase our awareness. We must open our eyes that we may see, and see that we may rejoice.

We must notice when prayers are answered and blessings

given. We must choose to see God and his work more often in
the work we do. We can see order and purity emerge as we clean.
We can see God's love and charity more clearly as we develop
integrity or practice peacemaking in the workplace. We can see
health and strength and vigor as we work or as we watch our children participate in sports. Watching our children grow and learn,
we can become aware of our own need to remain teachable
throughout our lives. As we become more alert to ways in which
eternal truth and spiritual gifts are inextricably woven into the
fabric of practical daily experience, we feel gratitude, wonder, and
joy. When we feel gratitude and wonder, we want to express it.
We find our thoughts turning to God with greater frequency.
Prayer fills our hearts until our days become one long, drawn-out
prayer filled with gratitude: *Sanctify my work, Lord, that it will bear
fruit. Help me with this, Lord, I'm in over my head.* And we grow in
grace. Our lives fill with grace. We become quieter, more centered, more grace-full.

As the awareness of God's grace increases in our lives, so does
our desire for service. Being more attuned to God, we become
more aware of opportunities for small acts of service, and we feel
prompted to act more frequently. If we respond to these promptings and act, we serve more. Gradually, we begin to offer all our
activities, at home, at work, and in the community, to God. We
slowly weed out those activities, thoughts, and responses that
cannot be offered to God. When we are conscious of his continual presence in our lives, unworthy thoughts and activities make
us feel uncomfortable, prodding us to do battle with our baser
desires and increase our righteousness. And we grow in grace.

The next step, after increasing our awareness and our service,
is to deliberately bring more of God into our homes and daily
lives: "These words, which I command thee this day, shall be in
thine heart: and thou shalt teach them diligently unto thy children, and shalt talk of them when thou sittest in thine house, and
when thou walkest by the way, and when thou liest down, and
when thou risest up." (Deuteronomy 6:6–7.)

We have family home evening and daily family prayer, but not enough of us do these things enough of the time. Even if we are doing these things, they are not enough. I would like to recommend to you a wonderful book filled with ideas for family traditions and celebrations that will help bring the Spirit into our homes: *Why Not Celebrate!* by Sara Wenger Shenk. The book is divided into four sections: daily rituals, weekly rhythms, yearly festivities, and celebrations for anytime. Mrs. Shenk is a Mennonite. In the introduction to her book, she eloquently makes her case for using rituals and celebrations in daily family life:

> I like to celebrate! At the same time, I'm not much for elaborate productions. . . . I know there are folks who have a flair for festivity, folks who can pull off an enormous bash and love every minute of the preparations. Not me! My style is to search for sacred meaning within the small, everyday moments, to revere the silences, the clasped hands, the broken loaf, the first evening star. One can compose a symphony of simple beauty out of the stuff that fills an ordinary day. By God's grace, that which is common becomes sacred and points to the reality of God in our midst. . . .
>
> Why have we forgotten that it is through our senses, all of them, that our hearts are enlarged so that God may enter in? . . . Our senses are the vehicles through which the Spirit of God enters into our constricted thought to make space for grace.[4]

In her chapter on yearly festivities, there are wonderful ideas for celebrating every event of the Christian calendar, the major Jewish holidays (Did you ever wish you could include a Passover celebration in your Easter traditions but didn't know how? It's here.), Valentine's Day, Mother's and Father's Day, and the last day of school. There's even a program in memory of Hiroshima that ends with the song "Let There Be Peace on Earth."

Imagine how enriched our personal and family lives could be

by adding just a few of these traditions and celebrations to our lives. "But we're already so busy," we think. We rush around from task to task with "to do" lists for one day that require two weeks to complete! How can we add anything to our already busy lives! In fact, many of these ideas are designed to help slow us down; others take little time and require little or no preparation. Let me illustrate with two examples, both celebrations of Christian seasons that Latter-day Saints, to our detriment, don't commonly observe.

The first is Advent. Advent is the first season of the Christian year and begins on December 1. Including Advent in your Christmas preparations is a wonderful way to slow down the Christmas rush and bring back a spiritual focus to a holiday that has become far too secular.

Many members of the Church begin their holiday decorating with the making of a wreath. In our ward, the Relief Society has a wreath-making party every year. This makes Advent an easy season to include in our family celebrations, and the wreath is a wonderful way to begin. We are all familiar with what the wreath symbolizes—the eternal circle, the continuation of life in the evergreen boughs. Knowing its history makes the symbolism even more powerful. The wreath, in fact, predates Christianity. It is borrowed. Gertrude Mueller Nelson wrote of this tradition:

> Pre-Christian peoples who lived far north and who suffered the archetypal loss of life and light with the disappearance of the sun had a way of wooing back life and hope. . . . Their solution was to bring all ordinary action and daily routine to a halt. They gave in to the nature of winter, came away from their fields and put away their tools. They removed the wheels from their carts and wagons, festooned them with greens and lights and brought them indoors to hang in their halls. They brought the wheels indoors as a sign of a different time, a time to stop and turn inward. . . .

Imagine what would happen if we were to understand that ancient prescription for this season literally
and remove—just one—say just the right front tire
from our automobiles and use this for our Advent
wreath. Indeed, things would stop. Our daily routines
would come to a halt and we would have the leisure
to incubate. . . .

Then the wreath is blessed: O God, by whose
word all things are made holy, pour blessings on this
wreath, our sacrificed wheel, and may it remind us to
slow down our hectic pace and make our hearts ready
for the coming of Christ your Son and our Lord. The
very sounds and smells help us to know that Advent is
here again. The story of Adam and Eve, the readings
from Isaiah and the words of John the Baptist are
familiar to us by now. We think about the days when
humankind had fallen from intimate "walking with
God," each of us aware in some way that we are
preparing for Him again to "come down and dance
with us."[5]

What a wonderful image of the sacrificed wheel! What would
our Christmas be like if we did all of our shopping, gifts, cards,
wrap, and errands before December 1. Then on December 1, we
hang our wreath, our sacrificed busyness, alongside an Advent
calendar. With the calendar we count the days, each day including a few gifts wrapped, a goody baked, some secrets kept, a scripture read, inching up to Christmas with an ever-increasing
spiritual focus. And we "make space for grace."

The second illustration comes from a season Latter-day Saints
completely ignore. It does not exist for us. In its commonly
observed form, I'm not sure it needs to exist for us, yet it has the
potential to bring increased continuity to our yearly celebrations.
The season is Lent.

For years, I have felt, and my children have expressed, the
sense of a gap between Christmas and Easter. There is an empty

space, a void. Christmas celebrates the birth of the Savior; Easter celebrates his death and resurrection; but when do we celebrate his life? When can we focus on his ministry and his teachings? Lent provides just such an opportunity. Lent begins six and a half weeks before Easter, on Ash Wednesday. We don't need to mark our foreheads with ashes and spend Lent focusing on ourselves and our shortcomings. Instead, we can use Ash Wednesday as a reminder that it is time to think about Christ's ministry. Introduce the season by reading the account of his baptism and his retreat into the wilderness for forty days of fasting and prayer. Then use the Sermon on the Mount for nightly scripture reading at the supper table. Even the youngest children and the busiest of families can manage to read, perhaps even memorize, one beatitude a night. The only preparation required is to put a Bible on the table with the plates and cups. By the time Easter arrives, you've spent four to six weeks with the Sermon on the Mount, and Easter has a whole new meaning. You and your family will feel more acutely the suffering and loss of the Crucifixion, the hope and joy of the Resurrection. But don't stop at Easter. Continue your nightly reading for a week or two after Easter, but this time, use the Book of Mormon and Acts. Read 3 Nephi with your children to build their testimonies of the risen Lord. Read the story of Pentecost in Acts to introduce them to the transforming power of the Holy Ghost. And "make space for grace."

These are celebrations of holidays—annual, occasional events. But what traditions, habits, and daily doings can be used to increase our awareness of God's presence in our daily lives? Almost anything will do—anything that stills you for a moment; anything that expresses love, compassion, or kindness; anything that honestly confesses weakness or uncertainty and thus opens up the possibility for growth. Many are things you are already doing—reading to your children, joining hands as you bless the food, taking evening walks, gardening together (or alone for that matter), having priesthood blessings when you or your children are sick—all open awareness and invite God into the realm of the everyday.

God's grace is all around us. His love is evidenced everywhere. As Paul writes, "I am persuaded, that neither death, nor life, nor angels, nor principalities, nor powers, nor things present, nor things to come, nor height, nor depth, nor any other creature, shall be able to separate us from the love of God, which is in Christ Jesus our Lord. (Romans 8:38–39.)

As we increase our awareness of his grace, as we celebrate his presence in our every day, we are moved to exclaim with the poets and mystics:

> All things were new; and all the creation gave
> another smell unto me than before, beyond what
> words can utter.
>
> (GEORGE FOX.)

> As to me, I know of nothing else but miracles.
>
> (WALT WHITMAN.)

> The clouds above us join and separate
> The breeze in the courtyard leaves and returns
> Life is like that
> So why not relax
> Who can keep us from celebrating?
>
> (YU LIN.)

Who indeed!

Chapter 9: Worship

Our Father which art in heaven, Hallowed be thy name.

—MATTHEW 6:9

A YEAR AGO LAST CHRISTMAS, we bought a beautiful telescope for our daughter. It was a little more complex than any of us cared to deal with, and we didn't have much success in finding anything but the moon. The moon is beautiful through a telescope, of course, but we soon tired of looking just at the moon, and the telescope sat unused in our back room for more than a year. Then just last week we were visited by an old college friend of my husband's. As it got late, he suggested we take the telescope outside and do a little stargazing. Our friend suggested looking at a particular star that was just rising above two trees on the horizon. As my husband looked through the scope, our friend eagerly asked if it was a star or a planet. My husband wasn't sure, so I looked. The object was larger and brighter than any star we had seen through the telescope before, and it had a kind of oblong shape to it. As I focused back and forth, I saw something else. "Oh my gosh!" I exclaimed. "I think there's a ring! Oh my gosh, there *is* a ring. It's Saturn!" I ran inside and shouted to my three children, "Hurry, come see. We've found Saturn!" Everyone took turns looking and exclaiming such adolescent superlatives as "wow" and "awesome." In between each child, I had to look again. I was like a kid myself, jumping up and down on my back porch. It's really true! It's really there! I'm looking at Saturn! The universe is really like the scientists say it is, and I can see it right here in my own backyard! *It's all so grand!*

The universe *is* a grand miracle, but we don't have to look into the depths of the cosmos to realize it. As we gaze into the heavens, as we enjoy the vast beauty of the earth, and as we enjoy our own health and growth, we realize that we live amid the miraculous. We are surrounded by the miraculous. We are infused with the miraculous. We are miracles ourselves. In *Our Town*, by Thornton Wilder, Emily speaks of the common miracles we enjoy everyday as she leaves the world to return to her grave: "Good-by, Good-by world. Good-by, Grover's Corner . . . Mama and Papa. Good-by to clocks ticking . . . and Mama's sunflowers. . . . . And new-ironed dresses and hot baths . . . and sleeping and waking up. Oh, earth, you're too wonderful for anybody to realize you." Then she looks at the Stage Manager and asks through her tears: "Do any human beings ever realize life while they live it?—every, every minute?"

"No," he replies. "The saints and poets, maybe—they do some."[1]

The saints and poets aren't the only ones; we can some too. As we think of human life and development; conception; childbirth; child growth and unfolding; how we can think, articulate, and share our thoughts one with another; our senses—touch, smell, eyesight; the balance between the sun, moon, earth, and stars, reflected on the minutest scale in atoms, electrons, protons, and even subatomic particles; and finally the gospel, the plan of salvation, the Atonement, and eternal life with our families and loved ones—as we think of all these things, we must realize there is nothing between Sunday morning and Saturday evening that is not wonderful and miraculous, and we sink to our knees in humble, grateful worship of our Heavenly Father. Worship is what our church activity must center around. Worship is what our lives must be about. How else can we respond to all we have been given?

Worship is both formal and informal, and I am afraid we don't do enough of either. I would like to examine our formal worship first, to look both at what's missing and what's there that we might use to improve our personal participation in community worship.

Worship and Sacrament Meeting

If one of your children asked you to explain the purpose of sacrament meeting, how would you answer? I have always heard that purpose stated as twofold: to partake of the sacrament and to learn more of the gospel. Worship is not usually mentioned. The fact that it is not one of the stated purposes of sacrament meeting does not mean it does not occur. Reverence is felt by many during the sacrament and during prayers. Praise is always expressed in our hymns and sometimes in the spoken prayers. Unfortunately though, for far too many Latter-day Saints, reverence is a fleeting and only occasional experience, and praise to the Lord is expressed only in song.

Adding to the problem that worship is not one of the express purposes of sacrament meeting is our suspicion of elaborate ritual and any language traditionally associated with it. Thus we come to regard the concept of worship with suspicion as we associate it with Catholic and Protestant traditions. If we examine this suspicion, we immediately realize how inappropriate it is.

In fact, we find examples of and admonitions to worship throughout the Standard Works:

> Worship the Lord in the beauty of holiness.
>
> (1 CHRONICLES 16:29.)

> I saw another angel fly in the midst of heaven, having the everlasting gospel to preach unto them that dwell on the earth, and to every nation, and kindred, and tongue, and people, saying with a loud voice, Fear God, and give glory to him; for the hour of his judgement is come: and worship him that made heaven, and earth, and the sea, and the fountains of waters.
>
> (REVELATION 14:6–7.)

> Worship him with all your might, mind, and strength.
>
> (2 NEPHI 25:29.)

You shall fall down and worship the Father in my
name.

(D&C 18:40.)

We don't fall down when we worship God in sacrament meeting, nor do we kneel when we say our community prayers. That
doesn't mean we can withhold our worship. Heads must be
bowed, hearts humble, and ears open as our public prayers are
spoken. Singing should be joined enthusiastically by all adults
and can be heartfelt and joyous. God's praises need to be thought
and spoken more during prayers and sacrament meeting talks. As
a church, we would be wise and, I believe, greatly blessed if we
stopped playing with our children during sacrament meeting, prepared our Sunday School lessons during the week, and came
together for an hour as a community to wholly and completely
worship God together. Done well and with meaning, this kind of
worship-in-community reaches deep into our souls, nourishing
our love for God and for each other.

Reverence

Reverence and worship go hand in hand, and reverence is
more than being quiet. The dictionary defines reverence as a feeling of profound awe and respect. A couple of years ago I was serving as a counselor in our Primary presidency. Reverence is a
common theme in Primary, and we discussed it often. One of our
concerns was how to help children realize that reverence was
more than just being quiet. We wanted them to *feel* reverence, to
feel profound awe and respect. I was asked to conduct a sharing
time on reverence. I had been taking a class on meditation and
visualization, and I thought a visualization exercise might help. I
approached that sharing time with more than a little bit of anxiety. I had never seen this kind of thing done in an LDS setting. I
wasn't sure how it would be received. Here is what the children
and I did.

First I told the children what reverence is and that we were going to do an exercise to help them experience it. I asked them to sit quietly and do everything I told them. (After you read through this, you might try the exercise yourself.) I asked them to close their eyes. Then I asked them to imagine themselves in the following scenario: You are walking down a path in a meadow. The meadow is filled with beautiful flowers. Birds are singing. The sky is blue and the sun is warm. You feel quiet and happy. As you walk, you realize that someone is approaching you from far down the path. You walk toward each other for a while. Now you can see him clearly. You stop as you realize it is the Savior.

He continues to walk steadily toward you. As he nears, you fall to your knees. He stops before you, reaches down to take your hand, and lifts you to your feet. Then he embraces you. As his arms fold around you, you feel his spirit wash over your entire body. He steps back, and as you look into his eyes you see his gentle love and concern for you. You stay there for a moment just looking into his eyes. Then, slowly, you turn and go back the way you have come. You walk back through the meadow and into your seats in this room. Now, open your eyes.

The room was totally still. Many of the children had tears in their eyes as I asked them to remember to take this imaginary walk with Jesus during the sacrament quiet time. I recalled with them the words to one of our sacrament hymns: "Jesus, the very thought of thee / With sweetness fills my breast."[2]

If we adults can also remember to focus our thoughts on the Savior during our sacrament meetings, both reverence and worship will become more common experiences for us.

Worship and Prayer

What does the Church teach about prayer? What do we teach our children about prayer in Primary? We teach our children and each other to pray using the following four steps:

1. Address our Heavenly Father.
2. Thank him for our blessings.
3. Ask him for the things we stand in need of.
4. Close in the name of Jesus Christ.

I have heard many talks given in Primary, sacrament meeting, and Relief Society on the subject of prayer. Many have used the above outline, but neither it nor any of the talks or lessons I've heard have ever mentioned worship or praise as being an important part of prayer. Now let's look at what the Savior taught about prayer. His teaching was done through a single powerful example:

> Our Father, which art in heaven
> Hallowed be thy name.
> Thy kingdom come.
> Thy will be done in earth, as it is in heaven.
> Give us this day our daily bread.
> And forgive us our debts,
> As we forgive our debtors.
> And lead us not into temptation,
> But deliver us from evil:
> For thine is the kingdom, and the power, and the glory,
> for ever.
> Amen.
>
> (MATTHEW 6:9–13.)

What steps does the Savior's prayer follow? I've counted six. First he addresses our Heavenly Father. We got that one right! What comes next? Hallowed be thy name: worship and praise. Third, he surrenders himself to God's will. Fourth and fifth, he asks for those things he stands in need of—first physical needs and second protection from the adversary. Sixth and closing is pure worship and praise, celebrating his Heavenly Father. Twice, at the beginning and the end, we find simple yet powerful expressions of worship and praise. I believe we would find our prayers more meaningful and our spiritual lives deeply enriched if we followed the Savior's example more closely, including expressions of praise in both our public and our private prayers.

It is important to distinguish the difference between praise and thanksgiving. Gratitude and thanksgiving often lead to praise, but they are not the same as praise. To say "Thank you for my many blessings" is quite different from saying "Praise the Lord!" or "Hallelujah!" All of our scriptures are filled with examples of people singing, shouting, and praying praises to God. Journals of pioneers from the early days of the Church are also filled with expressions of praise to God. It seems contemporary Saints have become too sophisticated or too dignified to exclaim praises to God in either public or private prayers. The language of praise is language that sounds unnatural to us. We are simply not comfortable exclaiming, as Mary did in Luke 1:46, "My soul doth magnify the Lord," or as David did in Psalm 103:1, "Bless the Lord, O my soul: and all that is within me, bless his holy name." We may never be comfortable with language that has become associated in contemporary times with excessively emotional, even hysterical religiosity. However, if we abandon the language of praise altogether, relegating it only to worship in song, we are making a terrible mistake. We can keep our praise within the framework of dignity and restraint, but we still need to express it.

When I first joined the Church, there was a man in our congregation who began each of his prayers with dignified praise. He did it by beginning all of his prayers with the first two phrases of the Lord's prayer, "Our Father which art in heaven, hallowed be thy name." He would then pause for a moment, and in the silence of that pause I invariably felt a deep sense of reverence. His prayers then proceeded in the usual fashion, giving thanks and asking for blessings. Using the first two lines of the Lord's prayer or something similar such as "Dear Heavenly Father, praise be unto thee" to begin our prayers brings an immediate sense of just who we are addressing and puts us in a worshipful and receptive frame of mind for the rest of the prayer.

If we study the Magnificat in Luke 1:46–55 or any of the

Psalms, we find a pattern in the way praise was offered to the Lord in biblical times. First are the exclamations of simple praise to the Lord. These are just an introduction and usually occupy only one or two verses. Following the exclamations of praise is a litany of the wonderful works of God, the glories of the creation, or a listing of specific ways the Lord blesses his people in general or the speaker in particular. This is another way we can increase our praises to the Lord in our prayers and particularly in our testimonies. When we bear testimony to one another, we need to do more than tell each other what we know to be true. We need to tell each other why and how we know it. We need to tell each other the ways God has been blessing us in our lives—the pain that was eased, the adversity that taught a valuable lesson, the problem solved. Describing to each other, in testimony, the ways Heavenly Father has been involved with our lives results in a litany of God's good works—the kind of praise and worship found in the scriptures. The language of praise needs to be our language, and words of praise should be on our lips and in our hearts whenever we address the Lord and often when we converse with each other. I would like to challenge you to incorporate more praise into your spiritual life. I would like to challenge you to refuse to allow yourself to present petitions or requests to the Lord until *after* you have uttered words of praise. I would like to challenge you to never end your prayers and rise from your knees without first praising your Heavenly Father. And I would like to challenge you to include a litany of praise to your Heavenly Father with every testimony you bear. I am convinced that if we do these things, our worship will be more meaningful and our blessings magnified.

Worship and Scripture Study

Have you ever worshiped God as you read the scriptures? You probably have, though you may not have realized it.

The General Authorities have often counseled us to ponder

the scriptures. For a long time I wasn't sure just what that meant. I decided pondering meant meditating, and meditating meant thinking about what I was reading—trying to figure it all out. Then I read a quotation from President David O. McKay: "Meditation is the highest activity of the soul." Hmmm. Figuring something out or thinking about it didn't seem to me to be the highest activity of the soul. I was missing something here. Then I read the wonderfully simple words of Robert Fulgham: "To ponder . . . is to wonder at a deep level."[3]

To wonder deeply. To wonder can mean two different things: (1) to wonder *about*—to try to figure it all out and (2) to wonder *at*—to stand in awe of—to worship.

It's happened to all of us, reading a particular verse or chapter; we've read it before but somehow it never struck us so hard before. But now—the heart stops—the figuring out stops—we're left breathless, speechless, for words cannot express the experience. For the moment we are still, knowing, intimate, with God. And we worship. We worship with more than words. We worship with our whole being.

Sara Wenger Shenk wrote of this act of worship:

> Opening oneself to wonder . . . is one of the best ways I know of cultivating the presence of God. Without the ability to wonder, all things become commonplace. But, when we open ourselves to wonder, everything is potentially sacramental. . . .
>
> . . . Being alive to the world nurtures a spirit of worship. By entering into the mystery of "how could this be," we embark on an adventure along a wonder-strewn pathway toward infinity.[4]

Other thoughts apply here as well: "The sound stops short, the sense flows on." (Chinese saying.) "Be still, and know that I am God." (Psalm 46:10.)

Worship and Daily Living

The experience described above is not limited to scripture study, prayer, or temple attendance. Throughout this book, I have described how the mundane events of daily living can bring us face-to-face with God. At times I have been stopped in my tracks, emptied, stilled, even stunned—in my living room, in my backyard, at work—shaking my head in wonder at grace expressed in my co-workers' lives, looking into the eyes of my children and husband, working in my kitchen, or driving in my car. I hope you have too. For as we see the Lord and his attributes expressed around and in us and in others, as we understand and appreciate more fully the complex and wonderful creation that we are a part of, we develop a sense of awe and wonder, an attitude of humility and worship, throughout our day. This growing experience has been described by Michael Stark and Michael Washburn as "the perception of the miraculous":

> Miraculous here refers not only to extraordinary phenomenon but also to the common place, for absolutely anything can evoke this special awareness provided that close enough attention is paid to it. Once perception is disengaged from the domination of preconception and personal interest, it is free to experience the world as it is in itself and to behold its inherent magnificence. . . .
>
> Perception of the miraculous requires no faith or assumptions. It is simply a matter of paying full and close attention to the givens of life, i.e., to what is so ever-present that it is usually taken for granted. The true wonder of the world is available everywhere, in the minutest parts of our bodies, in the vast expanse of the cosmos, and in the intimate connectedness of these and all things. . . . We are part of a finely balanced eco-system in which interdependency go hand in hand with individuation. We are all individuals,

but we are part of a greater whole, united in something vast and beautiful beyond description.
Perception of the miraculous is the subjective essence
of self-realization, the root from which man's highest
features and experiences grow.[5]

Words cannot describe the joy we feel when we learn to see
the vast and the beautiful in our daily lives. Each time we perceive the miraculous, each time we appreciate beauty, each time
we feel love, each time our problems result in our personal
growth, each time we experience strength or creativity in our
work, each breath we take, each step we walk presents us with
manifestations of the grace, the goodness, and the greatness of our
Heavenly Father. Worship him.

Worship him with words of gratitude and praise but worship
him with your actions also. We have discussed worship with
words. We have discussed worship with wonder. Now I would like
to discuss worship with actions, not just the service actions that
we normally think we can offer to God, but all of our actions. I
would like to discuss consecration. To consecrate means to give
all that we have and do to God. Consecration of our life to God is
the only response possible for those who truly perceive God's
goodness: "Thou shalt love the Lord thy God with all thy heart,
and with all thy soul, and with all thy mind. This is the first and
great commandment." (Matthew 22:37–38.)

To consecrate our lives to God means we value nothing more
than we value him and his service: "Seek ye first the kingdom of
God, and his righteousness." (Matthew 6:33.)

To consecrate our lives to God means we have no priority
higher than knowing and serving and becoming one with God:
"Though we walk in the flesh, we do not war after the flesh: (For
the weapons of our warfare are not carnal, but mighty through
God to the pulling down of strong holds;) Casting down imaginations, and every high thing that exalteth itself against the
knowledge of God, and bringing into captivity *every thought* to

the obedience of Christ." (2 Corinthians 10:3–5; emphasis added.)

To consecrate our lives to God means to bring every thought to the obedience of Christ. Consecration invites Christ to walk with us through our daily days. Consecration invites Christ into our jobs, our housework, our parenting, our marriages, our friendships and our church and community service. Consecration sees Christ and godliness expressed in our jobs, our housework, our parenting, our marriages, our friendships, and our service. Consecration surrenders all to God and sees God in everything and everywhere. Consecration makes each moment of our lives moments of worship. Consecration sanctifies our life and makes it holy.

Sara Wenger Shenk explains:

> I want to breathe in fresh air, bandage a bleeding knee, pick up trash around the neighborhood, cook a meal and know that what I do is all done for the love of God.
>
> Our favorite distinctions between sacred and secular are generally unhelpful. We cannot divide the spiritual from the practical. We are amphibious beings, creatures of spirit and of sense. It is through all the circumstances, inward and outward, that we are fed supernatural food.
>
> With a little discipline we can learn to offer our activities, small and large, to God, doing what we would normally do but doing it for God.
>
> As we do for God's sake what we normally do for ourselves, each deed, no matter how mundane, can become an act of worship.[6]

The Apostle Paul wrote, "Brothers, I call upon you, by the mercies of God, to present your bodies to him, a living, consecrated sacrifice, well-pleasing to God—for that is the only kind of worship which is truly spiritual." (Romans 12:1, Revised Standard Version.)

In his commentary on the book of Romans, William Barclay discusses daily consecration as he interprets this verse:

> "So," Paul says, "take your body; take all the tasks that you have to do every day; take the ordinary work of the shop, the factory, the shipyard, the mine; and offer that as an act of worship to God." The word in verse 1 which we, along with the Revised Standard Version have translated *worship*, has an interesting history. It is *latreia*, the noun of the verb *latreuein*. Originally, *latreuein* meant *to work for hire or pay*. It was the word used of the labouring man who gave his strength to an employer in return for the pay the employer would give him. . . . It then came to mean quite generally *to serve*; but it also came to mean *that to which a man gives his whole life*. For instance, a man could be said *latreuein kallei*, which means *to give his life to the service of beauty*. In that sense, it came very near meaning *to dedicate one's life to*. Finally, it came to be the word distinctively used *of the service of the gods*. In the Bible it never means human service; it is always used *of service to and worship of God*.
>
> Here we have a most significant thing. True worship is the offering to God of one's body, and all that one does every day with it. Real worship is not the offering to God of a liturgy, however noble, and a ritual, however magnificent. *Real worship is the offering of everyday life to him*; not something transacted in a church, but something which sees the whole world as the temple of the living God.[7]

William James said, "God and man have business together." We do. The issues of life are God's issues. Everyday life, everyday tasks, everyday worries and concerns, everyday triumphs and despairs, everyday lessons and learning, everyday moments, no matter how mundane, all belong to God.

It is with food, the pen, the hammer, the mop, and the

checkbook; in the kitchen and in the office, in the yard and in the living room; with the child, with the boss, with the neighbor that we truly worship God and our hearts, minds, souls, and lives are sanctified.

If we allow it, our everyday days are holy days, our everyday nights are holy nights, and our everyday life is truly holiness to the Lord.

NOTES

Chapter 1: Work

1. Studs Terkel, *Working* (New York: Pantheon Books, 1974), p. xi.
2. Victor L. Brown, Jr., *Human Intimacy* (Salt Lake City: Publisher's Press, 1990), pp. 104-5.
3. Bruce R. McConkie, *Mormon Doctrine*, 2nd. ed (Salt Lake City: Bookcraft, 1966), p. 847.
4. Hugh Nibley, *Old Testament and Related Studies* (Salt Lake City: Deseret Book and FARMS, 1986), pp. 112–13.
5. Anne Morrow Lindberg, *Gift from the Sea* (New York: Random House, 1978).
6. Benjamin Hoff, *The Tao of Pooh* (New York: New American Library, 1982).
7. Ibid.
8. Polly Berien Berends, *Whole Child/Whole Parent* (New York: Harper and Row, 1987).

Chapter 2: Ourselves

1. "Lead, Kindly Light," *Hymns of The Church of Jesus Christ of Latter-day Saints* (Salt Lake City: The Church of Jesus Christ of Latter-day Saints, 1985), no. 97.
2. Erich Fromm, *You Shall Be as Gods* (New York: Holt, Rinehart and Winston, 1966), pp. 54–55.
3. Meister Eckhart, in Berends, *Whole Child/Whole Parent.*
4. Howard Thurman, *For the Inward Journey* (Orlando: Harcourt Brace Jovanovich, 1984), pp. 61–62.

Chapter 3: Marriage

1. M. Scott Peck, *The Road Less Traveled* (New York: Simon and Schuster, 1978), pp. 81–83.
2. Brown, *Human Intimacy*, p. 125.
3. William Faulkner, in Stephen B. Oates, *William Faulkner: The Man and the Artist* (New York: Harper and Row, 1987), p. 249.
4. Brown, *Human Intimacy*.

Chapter 4: Parenting

1. Nibley, *Old Testament and Related Studies*, p. 76.
2. William Shakespeare, *As You Like It*, act 3, scene 2.
3. Berends, *Whole Child/Whole Parent*.
4. Sherrie Johnson, *Spiritually Centered Motherhood* (Salt Lake City: Bookcraft, 1983), p. 3.
5. Ibid., pp. 6–7; emphasis added.
6. Margery Williams, *The Velveteen Rabbit* (Garden City, N.Y.: Doubleday and Co.), pp. 16–17.

Chapter 5: Friendship

1. Ralph Waldo Emerson, "Friendship," *Essays* (New York: Merrill and Baker, n.d.), p. 132.
2. Anaïs Nin, in *Victoria Book of Days* (New York: Hearst Books, 1989), p. 29.

Chapter 6: Repentance

1. T. S. Eliot, *Murder in the Cathedral* (New York: Harcourt, Brace and World, 1935), pp. 30, 39–40.
2. *Lectures on Faith*, pp. 7, 11.
3. Peck, *The Road Less Traveled*, p. 273.
4. C. S. Lewis, *The Screwtape Letters* (New York: Macmillan Publishing Co., 1961), pp. 69–70.

Chapter 8: Grace

1. McConkie, *Mormon Doctrine*, p. 338.
2. Peck, *The Road Less Traveled*.
3. Sara Wenger Shenk, *Why Not Celebrate!* (Intercourse, Penn.: Good Books, 1975), p. 17.
4. Ibid., pp. 1–2, 9.

5. Gertrude Mueller Nelson, *To Dance with God* (New York: Paulist Press, 1986), pp. 64–64.

Chapter 9: Worship
1. Thornton Wilder, *Our Town* (New York: Harper and Row, 1957), p. 100.
2. "Jesus, the Very Thought of Thee," *Hymns*, no. 141.
3. Robert Fulgham, *It Was on Fire When I Lay Down on It* (New York: Villard Books, 1989), p. 59.
4. Shenk, *Why Not Celebrate!* p. 18.
5. Michael Stark and Michael Washburn, "Beyond the Norm: A Speculative Model of Self-Realization," *Journal of Religion and Health* 16:58–59.
6. Shenk, *Why Not Celebrate!*
7. William Barclay, *The Daily Study Bible Series: The Letter to the Romans* (Philadelphia: Westminster Press, 1975), pp. 156–57.

INDEX